January & February, 2016
Volume 1
Daily Devotional For Christian Businessmen

Sam Aihimegbe

2016 Daily Devotional For Christian Business Men and Women
Sam Aihimegbe @2016
ISSN 978-1-329-79822-9

A publication of Zion Gate Ministry Inc
CITEC Estate Airport Road, FCT, Abuja
Tel: 07056652694, 08141967026

Published by MasRose Media Ltd
Sam Aihimegbe @2016

E published From Nigeria By
Afrowebit.com
+234 (0) 80888 1 7777
www.afrowebit.com

Published & Sold Worldwide By
Lulu Press Inc, USA

Partner Today!

God is looking for your kind that is willing to take the gospel everywhere. You can sponsor a copy of this devotional and reach others that maybe in need of it.

PATNERSHIP LEVEL

Please indicate your partnership level, tick as appropriate.

GENERAL: Partner with any sum

SILVER: N8, 000 monthly, or N90, 000 yearly, and receive 50 copies

GOLD: N16, 000 monthly, or N180, 000 yearly, and receive 100 copies monthly

PLATINUM: N20, 000 monthly, or N240, 000 yearly, and receive 150 copies monthly.

Make all payments in favour of Sam Aihimegbe, ACC NO: 2018765373, UBA BANK. If you cannot return this part of the form, do send a text of all the details above to 07056652694. You can call this number for Bulk Supply.

Partners Details

Birthday_____

Name_____

Phone

No_____

Email

Address_____

Contact

Address_____

Would you like us to distribute your copies?

Yes____No_____

To Hospitals_____Schools_____Hotels_____

_____Prisons_____Others_____

Happy Xmas and Prosperous New Year!
2016, promises a glorious increase in your life, especially in
your business, career and vocation!
remain blessed!

Introduction

This devotional is designed to be of help, for Christian businessmen and women that maybe facing dwindling business fortunes and therefore needs divine leading and lifting, through its daily doses of spiritual insight that can revolutionize their businesses and guide them on their daily spiritual march, towards the full realization of kingdom objectives.

The devotional is therefore a life-changer, top-notch inspirational book and a special spiritual guide, designed to stimulate overall benefits in God's word, and fulfill the desire to encounter power daily.

How To Use The Devotional

Read and meditate on each article in a manner that you are able to get the central thoughts in it. Underline aspects that relate to your current challenges in business and study them for a longer time in order to have for maximum impact. Read the scriptures in the 'further study section,' until they form the picture of your intentions each day.

You can split the daily articles into two; by reading half in the morning and the other in evening. Attend to scriptural reading carefully and split same in other to have the full picture of what God is saying in your heart. May you enjoy God's glorious presence, power and blessings, as you read this special package of God's word, while anticipating your breakthrough and next-level testimonies.

Sam Aihimegbe
Zion Gate Min Inc; 31 CITEC Estate
Jabi, Abuja

Tel 07056652694; 08141967026, Email:
samisegho@yahoo.com

Personal Information

Name
_____
Home Address
_____

_____
Home Telephone
_____
Mobile
_____

E-Mail Address
_____

Business Address
_____

_____

_____

_____

_____

_____

_____

Goals for the month of January

_____

_____

_____

_____

_____

_____

_____

_____

_____

Goals for the month of February

_____

_____

_____

_____

_____

_____

_____

_____

_____

_____

_____

_____

Daily Devotional For Christian Businessmen
A guide for spiritual and business testimonies

1st Thursday

"And the LORD God formed man of the dust of the ground, and breathed into his nostrils the breath of life; and man became a living soul."

Gen 2: 7

Breath

Nowadays, believers are able to impart the life-giving power of God that is known as virtue or peace, on their families, homes, businesses and properties; Jon 20: 21; *"Then said Jesus to them again, Peace be unto you: as my Father hath sent me, even so send I you.* It is the greatest secret of success and profitableness in business.

The power is a promise of God that Jesus fulfilled; Acts 2: 14-21.It is the perfect therapy for bitter business meetings, unenforceable business decisions, dwindling financial fortune and apathy from uninspired staff. Praying in an office before the resumption of official activities refreshes the atmosphere for work and improves general levels of commitment. You can't point at a carnal direction, if you are spiritually minded and has charismatic nature that inspires hope, confidence, commitment and peace. Attending to the spiritual needs of your staff can heal work-place challenges, depression, anorexia and exhaustion. It can create transparency, and lead to the confession of sinful actions that hamper businesses.

You don't need to set up a church in your business premises, but go out to your business today, completely filled with the Holy Spirit. Be ready to impart the Holy Spirit on your staff, equipment and office furniture by faith; Eph 5: 18; *"And be not drunk with wine, wherein is excess; but be filled with the Spirit."*

How do you animate inanimate things with the Holy Spirit? How do you breathe on invincible things like ideas, plans, thoughts, vision and new concepts, and make them to assume divine and lively forms? You have to be born again to do it. To call things that doesn't exist as if they do; to bring dreams into reality. You must believe in the Lord Jesus and envision how to have Him in your heart. You must keep carnal interests from your heart and concentrate on the Lord. Through breath-transfer, your personal effects like clothes, office furniture and vehicles, will contact divine power. They will heal men, fellow businessmen and your staff. That's how the clothes of Jesus healed a woman with the issue of blood; Mk 5: 25-30. I want you to read and meditate on that story today. Imagine that your seat, table and car have contacted power and can heal the sick. Believe they can. Yes indeed; they can, if you breathe on them; if the Holy Spirit is impacted on them by you.

Prayer line

Dear Father, as I receive the auction to cause changes in my life, family and business today, fulfill your divine promise to use me to cause changes in the lives of others, in the name of Jesus! Amen!

Further Study
1 Jon 2: 27, Acts 2: 1-4

1ˢᵗFriday

"And suddenly there came a sound from heaven as of a rushing mighty wind, and it filled all the house where they were sitting."

Acts 2: 2

Know the Holy Spirit

In whichever way, anointed believers or men of God are able do miracles, signs and wonders, with the help of the Holy Spirit. The Holy Spirit is the medium for supernatural expression. Businesses are becoming increasingly difficult to manage, because of current global recession. Economic crimes and dangers in doing business with strangers have made the Holy Spirit, a worthy companion in the life of Christian businessmen. Just as Peter detected the ant-Christ lie of Ananias and Sapphira, you can detect fraudulent business practices through the Holy Spirit; Acts 5: 1-11.The Holy Spirit is the partner you need at these difficult times where financial experts can't predict the trend of global economic stability. Ask God for the Holy Spirit if you don't already have it. It is what guarantees your ability to explore the awesome realm of supernatural brinkmanship.

Men of God stay in the presence of God until their bodies are filled with the Holy Spirit. Someone asked me how he can be filled with the Holy Spirit, and I said he should go and stay in the bosom of the father. That's where Jesus lives. Shower men with deep compassion and be moved to help those in need. Take time to do this every week in your private moments, and you will have a clear spiritual direction. Stay indoors; fast, pray and meditate on the scriptures. Isolate yourself from the drunkenness of this crazy world for a moment and you will be enlightened spiritually. You will experience the in-filling of the Holy Spirit, if you do what endears the Holy Spirit to men – witnessing, soul winning and acts of faith.

Don't exhaust yourself with strenuous, haphazard and needlessly busy schedules. Do what will enable you accomplish great tasks for the Lord Jesus today, as soon as you are less busy. In fact create time to meditate Holy Spirit and read scriptural passages that are linked to the Holy Spirit. Forget everything you are passing through in your business, and just go to Him with deep desire, commitment and unbridled faith. When Moses stayed long in the presence of God, the Holy Spirit radiated on his face until could steadfastly look at him; Ex 34: 35; *"And the children of Israel saw the face of Moses, that the skin of Moses' face shone: and Moses put the veil upon his face again, until he went in to speak with him."* The Holy Spirit inspires, provides timely prophetic words, and spirit filled actions that repositions businesses and sanctifies homes, business premises and families. Get acquainted with the Holy Spirit today, and do wonders.

Prayer line

Dear Father, I believe in your only begotten Son, the Lord Jesus. I also desire the power of the Holy Spirit that I may be a blessing to my generation. I also desire the gifts of the Holy Spirit, ask for knowledge in order to impact the Holy Spirit on my family, business associates, business premises and also do great wonders in your vineyard, in Jesus name! Amen!

Scriptural Study
2 Cor. 5: 17, Jon 6: 63

2rd Saturday

"Professing themselves to be wise, they became fools."

Rom 1: 22

Don't neglect your source

Once we are born again we cleave to the Lord without options. We don't again detach ourselves from the Lord or neglect the source of our lives like a fish out of water; and foolishly forsake the commands and blessings of God. Business or no business we are the LORD's. We must realize that the source of our power, being, wisdom and prosperity is God; Judges 16: 16-21.If we remain faithful to God, we won't be betrayed by crafty friends, fraudulent business partners or defeated by the storms of life.

Samson is a startling example of a reckless believer that divulged the source of his power; got detached from God, his divine source, and was defeated by an unbeliever; Judges 16: 21; *"But the philistines took him, and put out his eyes, and brought him down to Gaza, and bound him with fetters of brass; and he did grind in the prison house."* You must avoid this sad picture of Samson, as you embrace fresh blessings, auction and power from the Lord. Remain connected; don't look outside the Lord. He knows the challenges you are facing in business; he knows your dreams and aspirations. We build our business empire –power, keen spiritual perception and faith, when we are connected to Him!

Get your acts together by faith, and be attached to your source; Jer. 17: 5-6, says cursed is any man that puts his trust in man, and whose heart departs from the Lord. Stop trusting in your business partners, trust in the Lord! This is why scriptures says, only fools dispute the existence of God; Ps 14: 1. *"The fool hath said in his heart, there is no God. They are corrupt, they have down abominable works, there is none that doeth good."*

Your belief in the Lord must rob-off on you and speedily confirm His covenant promises in your business. Stop neglecting your source of power like what many world-grown intellectuals, atheist, free thinkers and religionists, who profess to be wise, by detaching themselves from God are doing today. Connect to your source and stop living in fear, failure and uncertainty.

Paul warned Timothy not to neglect his life-changing gifts that he received from God; 1 Tim 4: 14; *"Neglect not the gift that is in thee, which was given thee by prophecy, with the laying on of the hands of the presbytery.* When you aren't connected your neglect your gifts and drift out of favour. Just as you encounter power through being connected to God; you can also impact this same power by praying for others, the laying on of hands and soul winning. By being in God's presence, you are refreshed daily and empowered to excel in business. Jesus breathed on his disciples after His resurrection, in order to impact a special seal of empowerment, faith, divine activity, profitability, and ministerial success that was preparatory to the gift of the Holy Spirit; Jon 20: 22; *"And when he had said this, he breathed on them, and saith unto them, Receive ye the Holy Ghost.* 'Go to your source!

Prayer line

Dear Father, just as you breathed the 'breath of life' into me, and I became 'a living soul,' cause me to also receive the power to breathe on my businesses, finances, profitability, premises and staffs today; that you may insure my business against devourers, business loss, failure; in the name of Jesus! Amen!

Further Study
Gen 2: 9-14; Ex 12: 21-24

3rd Sunday

"Labour not to be rich: cease from thine own wisdom."

Pro 23: 4

Higher heights

As a child of God, seek God's tender blessings over your life, family and business. That is what Jacob did after he was favoured to have the birthright of Esau. He had a rough beginning but a glorious end. Despite being blessed by God, Jacob fought hard to succeed. He knew it was God that would bring him out of the doldrums of life, and sought the Higher Heights of God's blessings by faith. Today, you can relocate to God's divine heights, by taking God's blessing that are in the heavenly places in Christ; Eph 1: 3; *"Blessed be the God and Father of our Lord Jesus Christ, who hath blessed us with all spiritual blessings in heavenly places in Christ."*

By simply desiring these blessings of Christ, Jacob wrestled with an Angel and had a prosperous name-change; Gen 32: 24-30. Cornelius received the Holy Spirit for being devout, haven earned a reputation for giving gifts to the poor, praying fervently and showing unparalleled acts of worship to God; Acts 10: 21- 22; *"And they said, Cornelius the centurion, a just man, and one that feareth God, and of good report among all the nation of the Jews, was warned from God by an holy angel to send for thee into his house, and to hear the words of thee."*

This is what I want you to do in your current business plan, so you can get compelling and visible testimonies. Put God in the heart of the business plan and look out for positive changes by faith. Higher Heights begins with a vision regarding your business, your personal life and the blueprint of your family. Ask God for innovative business strategies like Jacob did so you can experience your next-levels; Gen 30: 41-42; *"And it came to pass, whensoever the stronger cattle did conceive, that Jacob laid the rods before the eyes of the cattle in the gutters, that they might conceive among the rods. But when the cattle were feeble, he put them not in; so the feebler were Laban's, and the stronger Jacob's."* Getting out of the doldrums of any business must be sure and certain, not left to conjecture.

Prayer line

Father Lord, guide me and bring me to the high places in Christ that I may experience your providence, gracious portions, next-levels, prosperity of my family and overall business success. Let your glorious lines of miracles, next-levels and double-portions, fall onto me in pleasant places, in Jesus name! Amen!

Further Study
Ps 27: 10, John 1: 12-13

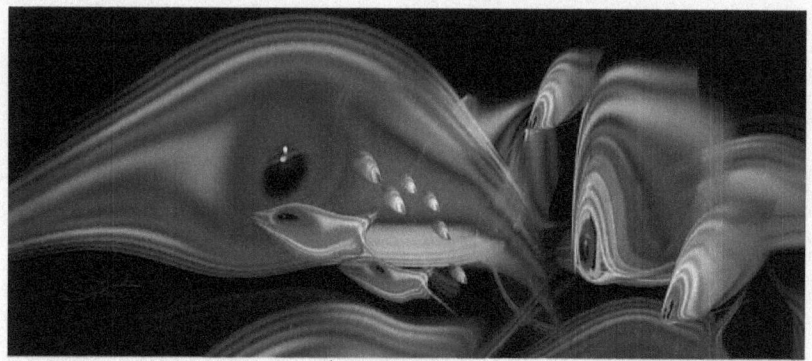

4th Monday

"He that goeth forth and weepeth, bearing precious seed, shall doubtless come again with rejoicing, bringing his sheaves with him."

Ps 126: 6

Break your lifetime of rigour

Life is not a bed of roses. Life is what you make of it. You must adapt to the demands of your business and ministry, and triumph over your challenges. Jacob adapted to a life of rigour, hard work and concentration; in order to break even. He also depended more and more, on God –on his vision, prophetic leading, and covenant promises. You can do same by faith. Establish some covenant promises regarding your business; and remind God of His faithfulness. In the course of his ride to the top, his unfeeling uncle Laban, who doubled as his father-in-law and master, changed his wages ten times; made him to work for fourteen years instead of seven, in order for him to marry Lear and Rachael, his daughter.Laban subjected Jacob to cruel servitude.Jacob was however determined to get to the height of God's divine blessing, and got there.

Jacob kept the vision he saw of God, dear to his heart. You must cleave to the Lord in order to get His divine blessings. The likes of David rose from obscurity, to international limelight, fame and stardom through the highway of rigor. Don't think life, ministry or business, is a bed of roses. It isn't. You must adjust to the demands of success, in order to succeed. Success demands that you're connected to God and work hard to succeed. Get a leading today and take up the full challenge of becoming who God wants you to be.

God blessed Jacob with a large family; he had healthy flocks, and was in good health, being an astonishingly rich business man like his grandfather, Abraham. Jacob's new height as a shrewd businessman made his uncle, Laban to envy him; Gen 31:1-16, When you seek God's higher heights, God's blessings and are in His good books, envy only promotes your overall prosperity and favour. You can break your life of rigour, nothing can stop you. All strategic decisions, all divine insight and goodwill are given by God, and revealed to you as a partner of His divine programme of eternal promotion, protection and prosperity. Jacobo beyed God's leading to leave Laban and go back home to his land; Gen 3: 13; *"I am the God of Bethel, where thou aniontedst the pillar, and where thou vowedst a vow unto me: now arise, get thee out from this land, return unto the land of thy kindred."*

Take stock of his confession of God's help, in the succeeding verses; and see that Jacob's overall success in business was divinely imparted. Note that it was solely based on God's decision to break his life of rigour, subjection and mortal enslavement. You can key into these special verses and also change the dwindling trend of your business; Gen

31: 8; *"If he said thus, The speckled shall be thy wages; then all the cattle bare speckled: and if he said thus, The ring straked shall be thy hire; then they bare all the cattle ring straked. Thus God has taken away the cattle of your father, and given them to me."*

Prayer line

O Lord, my God; cause my business to prosper this day, and make me a prosperous man. Let all my partners, bankers, financial sources approve my request for speedy support for higher heights, and insurance that my business will expand this New Year, grow and come to heights of profitability, fruitfulness and expansion before the end of this year, in the name of Jesus, Amen.

Further Study
Gen 30: 27, Gen 39: 1-6

5th Tuesday

"And Araunah said unto David, let my Lord the King take and offer up what seemeth good unto him: behold, here be oxen for burnt sacrifice, and threshing instruments and other instruments of the oxen for wood. All these things did Araunah, give unto the King. And Araunah said unto the King; the Lord thy God accept thee. And the King said unto Araunah, Nay; but I will surely buy it of thee at a price: neither will I offer burnt offerings unto the Lord my God of that which doth cost me nothing. So David bought the threshing floor and the oxen for fifty shekels of silver."

1 Sam 24: 22-25

Cost Everything

Follow the example of David and buy everything at a price. Don't look for gifts and profits at the same time. That's how to takeover the soul of your business. There is no proof that when we receive from others we will be blessed. Rather it is the other way round. When we give to others, we will abound in plenty and will be blessed; Luke 6: 38; *"Give and it shall be given unto you; good measure, pressure pressed down, and shaken together, and running over, shall men give into your bosom, For with the same measure that ye mete withal it shall be measured to you again.* It is more blessed to give than to receive. Make this mystery the soul of your business. Read this parable in Luke 13: 6-9, and find a crucial lesson for your business enablement. *"He spake also this parable; a certain man had a fig tree planted in his vineyard; and he came and sought fruit thereon, and found none. Then said he unto the dresser of his vineyard, Behold these three years I come seeking fruit on this fig tree, and find none: cut it down; why cumbereth it the ground? And he answering said unto him, Lord, let it alone this year also, till I shall dig about it, and dung it: and if it bear fruit, well: if not, then after that thou shalt cut it down."*

What do you make of this parable? The fig tree is your business. There are times when businesses experience low turnouts and loss of clientele. At such moments we will be tempted to abandon such business and do some other things. Whereas all we truly need is to dung it; empower it to grow and spread it or cause it to expand through the Spirit. All we need to know is God's word. Instead being frustrated we must learn to cast our burdens on the Lord and seek his face; 2 Chr. 7: 14.

It is an attitude that gives you a promising business altitude. Look at your business operations and block every waste and leakages. Get to your offices early and stay up late. Supervise your staff rigorously, and ensure they get their wages promptly. No work, no pay. As soon as your staffs have worked for the month, they must be paid. Don't delay salaries for an hour; James 5: 4; *"Behold the hire of the labourers who have reaped down your fields, which is of you kept back by fraud, creith: and the cries of them which have reaped are entered into the ears of the Lord of Saboath.* Nothing should be free; account for everything. Pay for every single service, and know that even your salvation was bought at a price!

Prayer line

Father Lord, thank you for giving me sound business strategy, ideas and ingenuity for my overall upkeep, business profitability and blessing. O Lord, teach me to be cost effective and prudent in business in Jesus name! Amen!

Scriptural Study
James 5: 11, 1Pet 2:7-10

6th Wednesday

"And Ruth said, Entreat me not to leave thee, or to return from following after thee: for whither thou goest, I will go: and where thou lodgest, I will lodge: thy people shall be my people, and thy God my God."

Ruth 1:16

Gather the fragments

When we suddenly come to grief, we must quickly remember the Lord, gather the fragments of our lives, and cleave to Him by faith. Jesus told the heart-broken loved ones of the late Lazarus, whom he raised to life that they shouldn't worry because He is the resurrection and life; Jon 11: 26; *"Jesus said unto her, I am the resurrection and the life: he that believeth in me, though he were dead, yet shall he live: And whoever liveth and believeth in me shall never die. Believest thou this?"*

Learn to believe Jesus all the way. We must depend on Him more and more and find solace in His enduring love, care, promises and blessings. The story of Job and Naomi must remain the watershed of our lives, when faced with hear-breaking misfortune. While we pray against such distresses, we must be mindful of the fact that the Lord decides what should be and not us. Our place is to go the way the Lord has prepared for us, by faith.

After they joined forces and fought some Kings of Canaan, and as part of the victorious party, the King of Sodom asked Abraham to partake in the spoils of war. Abraham declined: Gen 14: 2; *"And the King of Sodom said unto Abram, Give me the persons, and take the goods to thyself. And Abram said to the King of Sodom, I have lift up mine hand unto the LORD, the most high God, the possessor of heaven and earth, that I will not take from a thread even to a shelatchet, and that I will not take anything that is thine, lest thou shouldest say, I have* made Abram rich."Not all gifts increases wealth!

Prayer line

Father Lord, cause me to depend on you as my eternal source. I receive the auction for cost-effectiveness in business that I may experience your powerful blessings. Lead me daily that I may walk on the path of business success in Jesus name! Amen!

Scriptural Study
2 Kings 4: 38- 44, James 5: 17-18

7th Thursday

"If any of you lack wisdom, let him ask of God, that giveth to all men liberally, and upbraided not; and it shall be given him. But let him ask in faith, nothing wavering. For he that wavereth is like a wave of the sea driven and tossed. For let not that man think that he shall receive anything of the Lord."

James 1: 5-7

Be gifted

We miss the point when we fail to ask God for wisdom, in order to manage our business properly, expand our business through huge profit-margins, and record overall business success. This is what King Solomon did in 1 Kings 3: 5-10, and became the richest king in the world. He asked God for wisdom, after he sowed a historic seed that shook the heavens to its foundations. King Solomon offered a thousand bulls and God asked him to name whatever he desired.

Our primary desire should be to achieve sound business success. This must start from the onset of our business plan, not when we have gone astray, with our faulty business plans, and are stuck or have become bogged in huge business difficulties, stifling debts and our plans have failed. Before you ever set pen on paper, hold boardroom meetings, go to God in prayer and ask for wisdom, understanding and divine direction. We should ask God for requisite knowledge, skill and ingenuity in business, when we are just thinking of the business and are trying to put things together.

It was at this stage King Solomon asked God for wisdom and got it right; 1 Kings 10: 23; *"So King Solomon exceeded all the Kings of the earth for riches and wisdom."* Without divine wisdom you won't flourish in business. Go on your knees and ask God for it. God gave King Solomon robust business vision, competence and strategy that quickly enriched him; 1Kings 10: 27; *"And the King made silver to be in Jerusalem as stones, and cedars made he to be as the sycamore trees that are in the vale, for abundance."* This plummeted high lending cost, and increased private investment and trade.

In 1 Kings 10: 28-29, *"And Solomon had horses brought out of Egypt and linen yarn: the king's merchants received the linen yarn at a price. And a chariot came up and went out of Egypt for six hundred shekels of silver, and an horse for an hundred and fifty; and so for all the King's of the Hittites, and for the Kings of Syria, did they bring them out by their means.*" King Solomon was a business man who loved and greatly cherished international business and diplomacy. He traded in horses and Chariots and sold expensive robes and designer clothes; 1 Kings 10: 22; *"For the king had at sea a navy of Tharshish with the navy of Hiram: once in three years came the navy of Tharshish, bringing gold, and silver, ivory, apes, and peacocks."* These were bought and sold by the King.

Prayer line

Father Lord, bequeath your power of financial viability and wide-profit margin on my business that I may excel in my investment drive, in Jesus name! Amen!

Further Study

Job 5: 25, Ps 71: 19

8th Friday

"That the God of our Lord Jesus Christ, the Father of glory, may give unto you the spirit of wisdom and revelation in the knowledge of him."

Eph 1: 17

Business strategy

Strategy is another word for revelation; a special way to deal with problems, an easy way out of a complex problem. It is the secret of meeting huge financial targets. Revelation is what bequeaths staggering success in business. Go for it. The spirit of wisdom and revelation is central to your business prospects. There is no way a man can become rich without having a compelling business strategy that is tied to gifts of planning, business sourcing, partnership and growth. King Solomon sent his servants abroad, where they trained under experienced sailors, craftsmen and shrewd businessmen, from the cosmopolitan and commercial nation of Tyre; 1 Kings 5: 18: *"And Solomon's builders and Hiram's builders did hew them, and the stone quarers: so they prepared timber and stones to build the house."* He made an alliance with Hiram King of Tyre and this great King exposed King Solomon to the prospects, success and profitability of maritime business.

King Solomon's strategy was simple. He invested his presents, gifts and donations from friendly countries, kings and personages, and turned the windfall into robust and thriving businesses, especially; his export and import trade that flourished under God's leading. Ask God for such magnitude of business auction today, and be focused by faith. God is prepared to give you the gift of business success, strategy and overall wisdom, if you ask Him the way Solomon did, and rely fully on Him, for His providence. The Lord will teach you how to grow stagnant businesses, and break-even in profits, in order to excel in difficult business environments.

Understanding comes, when we show commitment to the trend of our businesses. When we strive to have breakthroughs and aren't slothful in business. Thirdly, we receive the gift of understanding, as part of our covenant blessing from God. It is the trait of our craftsmanship; Eph 2: 10; *"For we are his workmanship created in Christ Jesus unto good works, which God hath before ordained that we should walk in them."*

Prayer line

Dear Father Lord, grant me the wisdom and understanding, to deal with my challenges, in the name of Jesus! Amen!

Scriptural Study
Gen 24: 1,Col 2: 3

9ᵗʰ Saturday

"And he removed from thence, and digged another well; and for that they strove not: and he called the name of it Rehoboth; and he said, for now the Lord hath made room for us, and we shall be fruitful in the land."

Gen 26: 22

The art of business

Many don't know that Abraham made millions of dollars from the sale of water; Gen 24: 1; *"And Abraham was old and well stricken age: and the LORD had blessed Abraham in all things.* How did he make his money? He dug wells in strategic traveling routes, where many merchants transverse the land, and needed to water their camels and refresh themselves, before continuing in their desert journeys. Abraham keyed into this need, and made a fortune. It wasn't uncommon for him to buy goods off such merchants, and make supernormal profits, by selling it to nobles in neighbouring towns or cities. This way he was a renowned merchant. There are suggestions that Abraham also had a special tent to lodge stranded strangers for a fee.

Abraham soon made a fortune from his water and guest house business, before his neighbors began to envy him. They were afraid to challenge him because of his immense connections, wealth and might; Gen 13: 14-16.After the death of Abraham however, the Philistines attacked his business and covered his wells with sand. Isaac understood what that meant and clung to the first law of success in business: *"don't make enemies out of your business; make only friends,"* and decided not to confront them; Gen 26: 18-21; *"And Isaac digged again wells of water, which they had digged in the days of Abraham his father; for the philistines had stopped them after the death of Abraham: and he called their names after the names by which his father had called them. And Isaac's servants digged in the valley, and found there a well of springing water. And the herdsmen of Gerar did strive with Isaac's herdsmen, saying, The water is ours: and he called the name of the well Esek; because they strove with him. And they digged another well, and they strove for that also: and he called the name of it Sitna."*

Secondly, Isaac refused to give up on the family water business, despite the growing opposition and conspiracy he had to face. He has learnt the art of business from his father and there was no way he could abandon it; Pro 22: 6; *"Train up a child in the way he should go: and when he is old, he will not depart from it.* 'His family had a strong reputation for water business such that to do something else would be a huge loss of goodwill and sign of defeat. Thirdly it would be difficult to deploy his huge numbers of servants to any other business that may involve skills when his servants were grounded in the water business. Isaac put up another pressure to assert his business plan and dug the last well which paid off. Study how Isaac tied his prosperity to God's blessings! He had learnt the art of business from Abraham his father.

Prayer line

O Lord my God, cause me to understand the mysteries of the kingdom and learn the art of business today that I may avoid enemies in my area of business; help me to make friends, helpers and pillars in Jesus name! Amen!

Scriptural Study
Pro 5: 24-27; Pro 5: 15-17

10th Sunday

"Blessed Shall be the fruit of thy body, and the fruit thy ground, and the fruit of thy cattle, the increase of thy kine, and the flocks of thy sheep."

Duet 28: 4

Your business

Say it loud to yourself today that you're blessed. You are indeed blessed and are a blessing to the Church. You are blessed for being a child of God, and this blessing is boundless, as it reflects on your family and business; Gal 3: 13-14; *"Christ has redeemed us from the curse of the law, being made a curse for us: for it is written, cursed is everyone that hangeth on a tree. That the blessing of Abraham might come on the Gentiles through Jesus Christ; that we might receive the promise of the Spirit through faith."* You don't need to be anxious about the times and the current business environment, when you have received the promise of the Spirit. You're redeemed indeed. You're freed of trouble, of fear and failure.

Speak the word and hold on to the word of God by faith, and your heart desire will be met; Isa 54: 3-4; *"For thou shalt break forth on the right hand and on the left; and thy seed shall inherit the Gentiles and make the desolate cities to be inhabited. Fear not; for thou shalt not be ashamed: neither be thou confounded; for thou shalt not be put to shame: for thou shalt forget the shame of thy youth, and shalt not remember the reproach of thy widowhood any more."*

How do we overcome our widowhood? Is it through some sacrifices? No! We are blessed when we obey God. Deut 28: 1; *"And it shall come to pass, if thou shall hearken diligently unto the voice of the LORD thy God, to observe and to do all this commandments which I command thee this day that the LORD thy God will set thee on high above all the nations of the earth."* Learn to wait upon the Lord; the effect will show on your business. Moses waited on the Lord for forty days and forty nights and the congregation couldn't look at his face; Ex 34: 35. Moses had to veil himself because of the glory of God upon him. You can invest the glory of God on your business too! Go into God's presence right now, and get His glory on a platter of gold. Samuel told King Saul in 1 Sam 15: 22; *"And Samuel said, hath the LORD as great delight in burnt offerings and sacrifices, as in obeying the voice of the LORD? Behold, to obey is better than sacrifices, and to hearken than the fat of rams."*

Prayer line

Father Lord, grant me the power to obey you and receive the blessing. That my life, family and business maybe covered with your glory in the name of Jesus! Amen!

Further Study

Num 16: 23-30, Acts 5:1-11

11ᵗʰ Monday

"A false balance is abomination to the LORD: but a just weight is his delight."

Pro 11: 1

Some rules

Abhor deception, cheating and falsehood in business. That's what you need in order to excel and have breakthroughs. Deception turns off the glory of God, and brings the curse in your tabernacles. Don't use false weights and balances; Pro 20: 10. Strive as much as you can, to be part of the fellowship of God's children; Job 22: 21; *"Acquaint now thyself with him, and be at peace: thereby good shall come unto thee."* Don't lie or misrepresent your business operations, interests or any shady representation of your business.

Don't go on the fast lane. Your business will not expand if you fail to adhere to these rules. Hold on to your business by faith and grow it by adhering to the rules of increase. The first rule of increase is that you don't handle your business with a slack hand; Pro 10: 4; *"He becometh poor that dealeth with a slack hand: but the hand of the diligent maketh rich."* You must be diligent like the virtuous woman; Pro 31: 14-15; *"She is like the merchant ships; she bringeth her food from afar. She riseth also while it is yet night, and giveth meat to her household, and a portion to her maidens."*

Mr. K, an African immigrant, was a pharmacist based in the US. His business was buying medicines for private clinics across the US state of Nevada. He was given a rare appointment by the US government; what many immigrants sought with money. But after sometime Mr. K veered into the fast lane and began to defraud both the American government and the Association of Private Clinic Owners of Nevada. He began to falsify entries in the company lodger. When he supplied drugs for 50, 000 dollars, he will write 70, 000 dollars. He did this over a period of twenty years, until he was caught and arrested.

The FBI gave evidence of his long history of fraud, misrepresentation and stealing. He was tried and found guilty of fraud, stealing and criminal breach of trust, to the tune of two million dollars! The court asked him to pay the sum of two million dollars, and to serve a twenty years prison sentence. They stripped him of his license to practice pharmacy in the US, and told him he could face deportation after he has completed his prison sentence. It is a heinous crime to defraud the American state You must avoid a false balance and the fast lane; Matt 7: 13-14 *"Enter ye in at the strait gate: for wide is the gate, and broad is the way, that leadeth to destruction, and many there be which go in thereat. Because strait is the gate, and narrow is the way which leadeth unto life, and few there be that find it."*

Prayer line

O Lord my God; causes me to escape every snare of the fowler in the doorway of my business. Make me to see the tricks, traps and pitfalls the enemy maybe planning to bring on me today, in the name of Jesus! Amen!

Further Study
Eph 5: 3-5, Col 3: 3

12th Tuesday

"And he said unto them, How is it that you sought me? Wist ye not that I must be about my father's business? And they understood not the saying which he spake unto them."

Lk 2: 49

The master's business

You are indeed blessed for being a businessman. The master's business bears striking similarities with any business you are in right now. Are you in the business of buying and selling, or of rendering strategic services, for the upkeep and advancement of others? Are you an importer or an exporter? Are you in the business of training, building schools for learning, and supplying industrial machines for industries? Whatever business you choose, you are automatically linked to the Lord Jesus, when you do His business alongside yours. His burdens are light; Matt 11: 29:

"Take my yoke upon you, and learn of me; for I am meek and lowly in heart: and ye shall find rest unto your souls."The theme of this study is what the child Jesus told his parents when they looked for him for two days, and later found him in the temple. They met the child Jesus, as he sat and was taught prominent professors of the law. When they told him they were worried for haven not seen him for two days, Jesus told them they didn't need to be worried, as He had already commenced his father's business; the most valuable business of wining souls for the kingdom of God.

What have you learnt from this passage? *Firstly,* you must be found doing your business all the time, so that you are always busy, having satisfaction from doing what will make you advance the course of your business plan. What you should do in any case, is meet the Lord Jesus the greatest business innovator, creator and genius, so you can prosper, grow and expand the frontiers of your business; Matt 11: 28; *"Come unto me, all ye that labour and are heavy laden, and I will give you rest.*"That's what doing a business entails, going to cast the burden of your business on the Lord; Ps 55: 22.

Secondly, you must have creative power, knowledge in your area of business and requisite ingenuity. You must derive immense physical and mental satisfaction from doing your business; Eph 1: 17; *"That the God of our Lord Jesus Christ, the father of glory, may give unto the spirit of wisdom and revelation in the knowledge of him.*"No one grows in a business that he hates; in which he endures a great degree of pain, hurt and distress. You must have great staying power, in order to stay in business. You must be focused and not distracted in order to excel. Most people fail in business because they don't have innate skill, any diligent approach, innovative discoveries, or creative stimuli to be focused.

They have no staying power that's required to get sound business acumen, and expand the frontiers of their businesses. Scriptures says this capacity to be focused comes from the Lord; Pro 16: 1; *"The preparations of the heart in man, and the answer of the tongue, is from the LORD."*

Prayer

Father Lord, I want to thank you immensely, for putting the power of the Kingdom in the heart of my helpers. Let your kingdom nourish and direct the trend of my businesses, staff and financial needs today. Thank you for the anointing to serve you faithfully, and be a soul-winner. Thank you, O Lord; for giving me sound and refreshing business skills, for the ultimate growth and expansion of my business, in Jesus name! Amen!

Further Study
Matt 6: 19-20, Acts 10: 8-13

13ᵗʰWednesday

"And when the voice of the trumpet sounded long, and waxed louder and louder, Moses spake, and God answered him by a voice."

Ex 19: 19

The needful

You must know what you need most, in order to do the master's business. God wants you to make your request known to Him, so He can answer your prayers. That's the needful. The needful is what you need most in order to become proficient in business or ministry. What is the most important tool in ministry? The most important tool in ministry is that you must be born again. You must have a heart and mind-change that reflects the divine nature of God. Unless you experience this your business will never grow.

You must grow in the Spirit, and come to the understanding of the mystery of the fellowship. You must be an adept in prayers, holy conducts and knowledge of the word. You must be committed to soul-winning. You must be a practical Christian businessman. You must sow seeds and live by faith. You must acquire understanding from the Holy Spirit. You must be devoted to your business so that it shows in your profit margin;1 Tim 4: 15; *"Meditate upon these things; give thyself wholly to them; that thy profiting may appear to all."*

The needful is to hear God speak to your heart, and you obey. That is what is needed, for you to make high profits from puny investments. It is what needs to be done to avoid imminent collapse of your business. The Lord devoted Himself to His father's business and got a public declaration as the Son of God; Matt 3: 17; *"And lo a voice from heaven, saying, This is my beloved Son in who I am well pleased."* The Lord gave powerful teachings; preached to the low, high and mighty. He gave divine insight into His person and the power of the Kingdom. Therefore 'the needful' is haven to know the Lord; obey Him and acquire His mindset of meekness, mercy and love; Phil 2: 5-10.

The Lord Jesus was the centre of His Father's business. You must be the center of your own business too. You must personify your business and live by it. Because Jesus triumphed in His father's business, and His Spirit is you, you will not fail in your own business. The Spirit of Jesus that is in you will quicken your business and make it an astonishing success; Rom 8: 11; *"But if the Spirit of him that raised up Jesus from the dead dwell in you, he that raised up Christ from the dead shall also quicken your mortal bodies by his Spirit that dwelleth in you."*

As soon as you believe in Jesus, it setsthe tone of divine power on everything. There will be tremendous changes. When you make Him the author and finisher of our business, He will see to it that business succeeds. How will people regard your current business strategy, before it becomes visible? Have you laid it before the Lord in prayer?

Do you believe in it by faith? That's the needful! Now, get God involved in your business and relax.

Prayer line

O Lord my God; I sincerely desire that I be quickened by you, in order to grow my business, and experience all round over -flow in business and ministerial expansion. Guide me on this path of greatness and teach me your eternal secrets in Jesus name! Amen!

Further Study
James: 2:14-26, Titus 3: 7

14th Thursday

"See, I have called by name Bezaleel the son of Uri, the son of Hur, of the tribe of Judah: and I have filled him with the spirit of God, in wisdom, and in understanding, and in knowledge, and in all manner of workmanship."

Ex 31: 2-3

Your business style

Style is a special, easy way of doing something that maybe unique, difficult or complex. It is what bears the badge of your success in business. Sometimes we do business by creating a special effect in packaging or design of products or offering special delivery services that attract clients. Our approach to clientele relations, when we offer a new design of a product or brand our product or premises, often becomes the basis of the success story of our business. Style goes further than the targets of business success or product acceptance.

Style bequeaths a certain craze or special addiction in the psyche, hearts and conscience of clients that are moved by it. Style is the touch of elegance that distinguishes our businesses from others, and makes our creative efforts the ideal of a special talent. In business law, Style is the right you have over something, by which an infringement, can give rise to litigations. It is the prize for your special ability, talent and innovation. It is what creates the personality of any business. Success is reflective in the degree of mystery surrounding your style and product or service differentiation. That's why your business style also means your influence, guide, inspiration and overall skill over a business that makes it a staggering success.

Like the Lord did when he decided to create all the instruments of the temple, by investing certain individuals with the auction to do it, you must crave for the divine skill required for your style to lead to multiple profits in business. This will set you apart and bring you to the top of the business class. God listed certain aspects of style that you must learn in order to understand and achieve it.

First, you must have a personal relationship with the Lord in order to acquire style and become a genius; Jon 14: 23; *"Jesus answered and said unto him, if a man love me, he will keep my words: and my father will love him, and we will come unto him, and make our abode with him."* When we obey God's word, we're changed to reflect His glorious image. This is what brings the Lord into the fold of our business and we acquire His business strategy free of charge.

When He comes He teaches us, equips us and transforms us. It is being in God's presence that impacts business style and elegance. Like the Lord did to Obededom's household, when David abandoned the Ark with him for three months, and the Lord blessed him; the Lord will bless you if you remain in His presence and obey His words. This is what will take you to the top; 2 Sam 6: 10- 12. Talk to the Lord like a friend, and he will fulfill your heart-desire in this regard.

Secondly, you must be filled with the Holy Spirit, for your style to appear so that you can become consistent; Eph 5: 18; *"And be not drunk with wine, wherein is excess but be filled with the Spirit."* This also means you must tap your skill to the limits and stretch your imagination as much as you can for your business get off the ground and get to the height of relevance that you desire. That's how your insights, inspiration and goodwill can appear.

Prayer line

Father Lord, teach me a style that will make me surpass my equals in business. Teach me what to do that I maybe full of your auction for business proficiency, expansion and increased profitability, in Jesus name! Amen!

Further Study

Gen 24: 1, Jon 1: 51-56

15th Friday

"And Moses chose able men out of all Israel, and made them heads over the people, rulers of thousands, rulers of hundreds, rulers of fifties, and rulers of tens."

Ex 18: 25

Managing your business

Keenly understand every detail of your business; proposals, work plan, available investment opportunities and financing. Know how to meet the challenges of your management, and what's required to train your specialized staff in your new business strategy. This in turn bequeaths your business style and needed blueprint for success in business. The most important challenge in business is how to manage it properly, so you can break even, and make outstanding profits. That's your primary area of responsibility and also the greatest tasks. Ask God for a unique way to handle dangerous difficulties, decisions or complex choices in your business today.

God gives immense capacity to manage businesses, huge ministries or vast kingdoms, no matter how complex. He is a master-builder that offers diverse business strategies and administrative differences that strikes at the heart of mega businesses that have becomes household names, in their long years of maximizing profits and minimizing losses. God is the author of divine business tips that guarantees success in business management and ministry. Paul gave insight into his calling and taught the grace that God gave him, in order to excel in ministry. You can ask God for similar grace, in order to master your complex management tasks in business; 2 Cor. 11: 21- 31.

After Moses brought the children of Israel out of Egypt, he was faced with the task of ruling them. Unknown to him his father-in-law, Jethro studied him. Ex 18: 13; *"And it came to pass on the morrow that Moses sat to judge the people: and the people stood by Moses from morning unto the evening.* Jethro advised Moses to decentralize his administrative authority in order not to wear away the people and himself. In Ex 18: 25, Moses appointed able bodied men, and made them heads over the people, rulers of thousands, rulers of hundreds, rulers of fifties, and rulers of tens.

Prayer line

Father Lord, give me a special business style and uniqueness that will cause me to get to the top of my business career today. I crave your divine presence and glory, in all that pertain to my business in Jesus name! Amen!

Further study
Gen 4: 3-7, Gen 35: 1-13

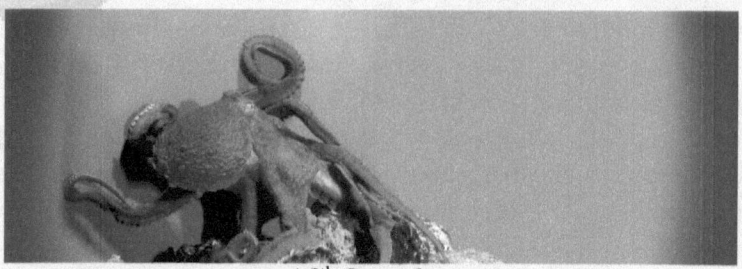

16th Saturday

"For wheresoever the carcass is, there will the eagles be gathered together."

Matt 24: 28

Grow your business

Growth is an aspect of life that is tied to God's favour and empowerment. You can only grow your business by learning your trade from the Lord Jesus; Matt 4: 18-19; *"And Jesus walking by the sea of Galilee, saw two brethren, Simon called Peter, and Andrew his brother, casting a net into the sea: for they were fishers. And he said unto them, Follow me, and I will make you fishers of men.* Fishing men by divine attractiveness grows your business. Your guide remains the scriptures and your power is the Holy Spirit. The moment you acquaint yourself with the Lord, He will teach you this great secret so that you may get your breakthrough.

Your background changes everything; 1 Cor. 5: 17. Growth and expansion must be the reward of haven been planted on fertile ground. When you were born again, you became a new creature that operates the law of the Spirit of Life that's in Christ Jesus. As a result of your divine nature you began to follow the pattern of success stories set by Christ. What's this pattern of business success or success story that stimulates divine attractiveness? It is the mystery of the buried seed that the Lord Jesus said multiplies after it has died and now springs new essence of life through the mystery of growth; Jon 12: 24; *"Very, verily, I say unto you, except a corn of wheat fall into the ground and die, it abideth alone: but if it die, it bringeth forth much fruit."*

Your understanding of how to strategize your business for maximum profitability or create innovative business plans that are foolproof, has to be broken, remodeled by the Lord Jesus and spiritually rebased. It has to be standardized by the quickening power of God. You will attests to this after you have acquired His divine nature which impacts His fullness; Jon 12: 24' *"Verily, verily, I say unto you, except a corn of wheat fall into the ground and die, it abideth alone: but if it die, it bringeth forth much fruit."*

In order words, your commitment to the Lord must be such that you are seeped in the power of the Holy Spirit, and walks steadfastly, under the principle and power of prosperity that's in the Lord Jesus. Being in the Spirit also gives the intuitive desire to obey the Lord's command and receive His blessings that are packaged, and relayed as soon as we see things the way God does; oriented to God's ways of doing things by faith; 2 Cor. 4: 18; *"While looking not at the things which are seen, but at the things which are not seen: for the things which are seen are temporal; but the things which are not seen are eternal."*

Prayer line

Father Lord; teach me how to grow my business today that I may encounter the mystery of growth in my life, business and ministry in Jesus name! Amen!

Further Study
Isa 62: 1-2, Eph 2: 8-10

17th Sunday

"Ye have heard how I said unto you, I go away, and come again unto you. If ye loved me, ye would rejoice, because I said, I go unto the Father: for my father is greater than I."

John 14: 28

Move on

Living in the Spirit involves systematic changes that confirm your next-level blessings, divine protection and prosperity. God loves progressive changes that show up in our lives and are designed to take us to higher heights, next-levels of prophetic expectation, where we can tap into the law of divine multiplication; Jon 12: 24. The will of God is that you should reap mega profits in your business and experience deep satisfaction from growing a successful business or ministry. This is a mystery. Your business will grow because you have imparted the life of God on it and have grown in the fertile ground of the Spirit; Mk4: 20; *"And these are they which are sown on ground; such as hear the word, and receive it, and bring forth fruit, some thirtyfold, some sixty, and some hundred."*

Your growth expectation in business is tied to your growth in Kingdom investments. Both are one. Just as Jesus directed Peter to fish in barren waters and caught a great haul of fish, so are you expected to use the power of the Kingdom, to saturate your business and reap huge profits? In order to move to the next levels, fulfill your vows; pay tithes, become visible in your fellowship and have a prayerful ministry. Whereas your kingdom investments are paramount to your excellence in business, your spiritual duty to God are fundamental to your overall success.

Secondly, if you don't move on from unfavorable grounds, you won't get your deserved rest unless it is in line with God's leading. Movement of whatever kind, when channeled properly, often breaks stagnation, temptation and persecution. When the Lord's business suffered a loss at his native home of Nazareth, he left there and never returned there to preach. In Matt 10: 14, he told the disciples; *"Whosoever shall not receive you, nor hear your words, when ye depart out of that house or city, shake of the dust of your feet."*

The Lord went to Capernaum and his business flourished; Matt 4: 13-17. He assembled his disciples and moved on; Matt 4: 18-25.Verse 25; *"And there followed him great multitudes of people from Galilee (Gentile territory), and from Decapolis, and from Jerusalem, and from Judea, and from beyond Jordan."* His ministry that faced shrinking fellowships and low turnouts in Nazareth, grew rapidly in Gentile territories, when he stepped his foot outside where He was raised. Don't waste your precious time over any problem. Find immediate solutions and move on. Paul talked about the things he had to leave behind, in order to press on (move on), and be apprehended by the engaging fellowship of the mystery; Phil 3: 13; *"Brethren, I count not myself to have apprehended: but this one thing I do, forgetting those things which are behind, and reaching forth unto those things which are before."*

Move on. Forget your shame, pains and the trend of former things. Forget the former things, as they have passed away. What is important is the present. Behold all things are now new. Stop banking on former friends, or promises of help, from family members. It may never come. Reach out to new faces and create new expectations. Be creative, be assertive; be expeditious. You won't get your next-level packages, nor reap double-portion testimonies, from the commonwealth, if you hold on to your past siege of false hope, heart -breaks and misery.

Prayer line

O Lord my God; cause me to experience all round growth today. Let me encounter the mystery of inward grace that creates the power of multiplication in Jesus name! Amen!

Further Study
Gen 2: 28-29, Gen 17: 1-2.

18th Monday

"In the beginning was the word, and the word was with God, and the word was God."

John 1: 1

Don't be a stranger

Greatness, increase, multiplication, growth, success in business, creative brilliance, effective use of talent or gifts; expansion in vision and prosperity, ultimately comes from God. Our scriptural text says; God is His word. God impacts His power, beauty and creativity on us, when we believe His word. He makes our families to grow in power, wealth and glory. He orders our grandeur and supervises our lifting. You can only become a great business man by reading, obeying and believing God's word.

By meditating on it day and night; Psalm 1: 1-3; *"Blessed is the man that walketh not in the counsel of the ungodly, nor standeth in the way of sinners, nor setteth in the seat of the scornful. But his delight is in the law of the LORD; and in his law doth he meditate day and night. And he shall be like a tree planted by the rivers of water, that bringeth forth his fruit in his season; his leaf also shall not wither, and whatsoever he doeth shall prosper."*

Obeying God's Word today and God will give you a renewed mind that channels the virtues, issues and potentials of God into your business; Mk 11: 23-24.Meditate on God's word, so that the Lord can bring you to your deserved season of prosperity, stability and growth. That's how not to be a stranger to the covenants of God. For instance Psalm 23: 4, says; *"Yea, though I walk through the valley of the shadow of death, I will fear no evil: for thou art with me; thy rod and thy staff they comfort me."* You are armed with the staff of breakthroughs and prosperity, if you take center-stage in the ministry.

Don't forget how Moses did the wonders of God, by using the shepherd staff in his hand. Get yourself a shepherd staff from the Lord by becoming a leader in your church. You must be a leader of the church in order to be a shepherd. Yes, to be able to lead the children of Israel, Moses had to become a shepherd. He had to be divested of his Egyptian mentality, or authoritarian upbringing, as Pharaoh's daughter son, in order to become the meekest man on earth. He tore off the clothes of a stranger and became the deliverer of his brethren. That's the transformation you need. Get rid of fear and how the world views your dreams or vision, and obey God's word.

Prayer line

Father Lord, give me the power to connect my business to your throne this day, that I may not be a stranger to the covenant of greatness in the life of your children in Jesus name! Amen!

Further Study
1 Sam 16: 14-18, Gen 32: 10-12

19th Tuesday

"If ye shall ask anything in my name I will do it."
Jon 14: 14

Direct your destiny

Don't leave your future to mere conjecture, ask anything in His name and get it right from above; Matt 18: 18; *"Verily I say unto you, whatsoever ye shall bind on earth shall be bound in heaven: and whatsoever ye shall loose on earth shall be loosed in heaven."* Your destiny is how easily you are able to bind and loose things that shape your future. Don't leave blank spaces in your life, fold your hands like a sluggard and ruin your future. Reject the nihilist philosophy of what will be, will be; and take charge of your destiny. It is nonsense to think that anything will make you succeed, if just sit somewhere, and not do anything about how to become successful. My friend, you are born to create a difference.

There are signs that should follow you. As a child of God you are born for signs and wonders. You have a hand in the fortunes or misfortunes of your future. If you have no hand in your future, why should you be held responsible for your sinful errors and be counted as a transgressor; Gal 2: 18; *"For if I build again the things which I destroyed, I make myself a transgressor."* There will be no need to beheld accountable for offences, when we are clearly incapable of controlling our destiny. Be bold to assert yourself today, and fight to change your future. That's the primary reason why the Lord Jesus came, that you be able to change your destiny; Matt 4: 16,: *"The people which sat in darkness saw great light; and to them which sat in the region and shadow of death light is sprung up."*

What is destiny? But actions, inactions, omissions and silly mistakes, like not doing anything about your life that collusively forges your future, especially when completely left untended and properly directed. Your choices, preferences and decisions and how they affect your fortunes in life. You can terminate the great or silly event that leads to the crisis or peace of your future. *I want you to know that your destiny is the realization of the future, which is borne out of the fulfillment of your direction, to which you must go, when properly channeled by you.* The forces that mould destiny are had out of personal pressure, desire, decision, choice and inevitable action. Understand that you have tremendous control over these destiny-molding forces that creates other phenomena like sin, emotion like anger, passion, love, hate, action or inaction.

The more negatively inclined you're in respect of these emotions, the badly driven your destiny becomes. The more positively inclined, the well-driven your destiny looks. Who determines your destiny in these circumstances? It is you that determines it. You are what you think; and will become what you do. You can change your looks if decides. This is how you create your destiny. Invincible forces bring tremendous pressure to bear on your mind. Your mind responds to such pressure through desire. Desire creates your personal decision to act on such pressure. That decision leads to either action; inaction or consummation of desire. You aren't forced to consummate your desire. In fact you can ignore your desire. But as soon as you consummate your desire through a certain action, it creates a particular direction known as destiny.

No one is destined to fail. Everyone creates the forces, excuses, mistakes, right judgment or misjudgment that pushes them off the cliff of success, into an abyss of failure. When God sent Elijah to condemn King Ahab for killing Naboth the Jezreelite, the King repented and God changed his mind; 1 Kings 21: 27-29. Read verse 29; *"Seest thou how Ahab humbleth himself before me? Because he humblet himself before me, I will not bring the evil in his days: but in his son's days will I bring the evil upon his house."*

Prayer line

O Lord my God; give me the innovative power your word that I may conform to your blessings and promise of prosperity. Teach me deeper mysteries of your Word today that I may grow my business, spiritually and physically, in Jesus name! Amen!

Further Study
Jon 7: 38, Jer. 1: 4.

20th Wednesday

"But they that wait upon the LORD shall renew their strength; they shall mount up with wings as eagles; they shall run, and not be weary; and they shall walk, and not faint."
Isaiah 39: 31

Your business

As a Christian businessman, you have no reason to fail in business. You have no reason not to stand out and call the shots in your business community. Abraham, Isaac and Jacob were outstanding Christian businessmen. They excelled in business and overwhelmed their times. To achieve this, you must follow the path paved by God's word, and learn how they mastered their challenges. You must follow the dictates of scriptures to the later.

Take your business seriously by believing in the Lord Jesus. Get oil on your business lamp, and let it burn; Matt 25: 1-13. Heed the warning in Matt 25: 13; *"Watch therefore, for ye know neither the day nor the hour wherein the Son of man cometh."* When we are ready all the time, we inevitably control the times. But when we wait upon Him, we will stand out in business and conquer the times. One way to have a lifestyle of business success, where we can't be wearied or troubled, is when the Lord becomes part of our business strategy, and leads in the direction of its sustainability and profitability. It is when we have a supernatural understanding of the times, by waiting upon the Lord; Isa 40:31.

The times hold the fortunes of any business. Businessmen dread evil times. And because the times aren't predictable, you must believe in the Lord, who is master of the times and get your breakthroughs. Your reward of discipleship comes from when you are both certain that God has approved your business at the right time, or has set a business timetable for you to accomplish. When your blessing is certain and you can vouch for it by faith, then you know that your time for your elevation in business has come. For you to have such insight today, and remain in faith, know the mindset of the Lord and execute it. The Lord has promised that everything shall be revealed at the appropriate time. There is nothing hidden that shall not be revealed. Don't neglect this insight into your future and the destiny of your business. Know the times; get a blue-print of God's word regarding your business situation and move on by faith.

Look at 2 Chr. 7: 14. It says; *"If my people, which are called by my name, shall humble themselves and pray, and seek my face, and turn from their wicked ways; then will I hear from heaven, and will heal their land.* Your business is to humble yourself and pray. Jesus said in JN 14: 13; *"And whatsoever ye shall ask in my name, that will I do that the father maybe glorified in his son"*

Prayer line

Father Lord, grant me the grace to succeed in business; the wisdom to excel in ministry and the power to obey your will in Jesus name! Amen!

Further Study
Gen 1: 28-29, Pro 12: 1

20th Thursday

"Looking unto Jesus the author and finisher of our faith; who for the joy that was set before him endured the cross, despising the shame, and is set down at the right hand of the throne of God."

Heb 12: 2

Look heavenward

The essence of your relationship with God, is to enable you look heavenward, when faced with challenges. So you can boldly say what the psalmist said in Ps 34: 2; *"My soul shall make her boast of the LORD: the humble shall hear thereof and be glad."* There are no solutions, when we look at men.

Our problems will multiply. Jesus taught that we should beware of men; Matt 10: 17; *"But beware of men: for they will deliver you up to the councils, and they will scourge you in their synagogues; and ye shall be brought before governors and kings for my sake, for a testimony against them and the gentiles. "*We shouldn't put our trust in men; Jer. 17: 5-6; *" Thus saith the LORD; cursed be the man that trusteth in man, and maketh flesh his arm, and whose heart departeth from the LORD. "*

The Lord Jesus hadlots of challenges but demonstrated His absolute trust in His Father, as an example of what we should do, by believing in Him; Ps 34: 5; *"They looked unto Him, and were lightened: and their faces were not ashamed. This poor man cried, and the LORD heard him, and saved him out of his troubles. The angel of the LORD encampeth round about them that fear him, and delivereth them. "*

In order to look heavenward, you must share in the mystery of divine love that's in Christ Jesus; Jon 10: 30; *"I and my father are one. "*In Jon 17: 3, the Lord Jesus described the content of this relationship as eternal life; *"And this is life eternal, that they might know thee the only true God, and Jesus Christ whom thou hast sent.* 'Looking heavenward and acquiring the mindset of eternity, involves being born again, the acquisition of the divine nature that proves we have defeated lust and corruption in our lives and businesses; 2 Pet 1: 4. It is proof of being nurtured by the Holy Spirit; or like scriptures said of Jesus in Lk 2: 52; *"And Jesus increased in wisdom and stature, and in favour with God and man. "*In which case, you must walk according to kingdom rules, and be engaged in kingdom activities; Jon 3: 16, Rom 8: 1-2.

You can be blessed right where you are, if you look heavenward, and execute His commands. When Isaac was faced with options of going to Egypt, God gave him a heavenly solution in Gen 26: 12; *"Then Isaac sowed in that land, and received in the same year an hundredfold: and the Lord blessed him. And the man waxed great, and went forward, and grew until he became very great: for he had possession of flocks, and possession of herds, and great store of servants: and the philistines envied him."*

Prayer line

Father Lord, bless me and turn my situation around. You can change my destiny and make it to reflect that of Abraham, Isaac and Jacob. Do it today O Lord, in Jesus name! Amen!

Further Study

Acts 6:7-8, Romans 4: 16-25

22nd Friday

"Drink waters out of thine own cistern, and running waters out of thine own well. Let thy fountains be dispersed abroad, and rivers of waters in the streets. Let them be only thine own, and not strangers with thee."

Pro 5: 15-17

Dig your wells

Set out your greatness through the path of hard work, creative vision, risk-bearing and sound financial management. Lookout for your talents, gifts and other spiritual endowments, and use them. You are the one that knows the way, be on the right track and become unique in your choice of business. In Gal 2: 4-5, Paul complained of certain brethren, who came to preach what was contrary to sound doctrine.

When you dig your wells, you will become conscious of trespassers. *"And that because of false brethren unawares brought in, who came to spy out our liberty which we have in Christ Jesus that they might bring us into bondage: to whom we gave place by subjection, no not for an hour; that the truth of the gospel might continue with you."*

A trespasser or stranger is someone that doesn't believe in the Lord Jesus Christ; 1 Jon 2: 15-17. He is a dangerous outcast that's outside the covenant terms of God. You have to be determined to outdo such trespasser by destroy his influence over your business and neutralize his fancies;1 Cor. 2: 3; *"For I determined not to know anything among you, save Jesus Christ, and him crucified."* A stranger or trespasser is someone with an alien disposition; someone that will never agree to be part of our bargain in life, business and ministry.

He is some one with a hostile, warlike, indifferent or contrary spirit. Jesus, while describing His disciples, singled out Judas as the weak-link; and called him 'the son of perdition;' Jon 17: 12; *"While I was with them in the world, I kept them in thy name: those that thou gavset me I have kept, and none of them is lost, but the son of perdition; that the scripture might be fulfilled."* The stranger will forever betray us, or 'lift up his wicked heel against us,' no matter how we try; Ps 41: 9. Jesus described them as those that are not gathering with him; those who are scattering abroad; Matt 12: 30.

In order to overcome the power of the stranger, learn to dig your wells. Found your business on the word of God. Let your business revolve round you. Be the boss and feel on top. I'm not saying you shouldn't mix with others or that you should isolate yourself. No! Let the soul of your business be under your control. Be the final authority; the absolute CEO! That's the essence of the text under study.

Prayer line

Father, Lord; make me a family like a flock. Fulfill your word concerning my life, family and business. Cause me to grow from my little beginning, until I am fully established. I refuse to give up or hand my providence to strangers in Jesus name! Amen!

Further Study
Gen 40:6, Ex 22: 20

23rd Saturday

"And I will bless them that bless thee, and curse him that curseth thee: and in thee shall all the families of the earth be blessed."

Gen 12: 3
Bless others

Let thy fountains be dispersed abroad; running water in the streets. You should come to a stage in life, where you become a blessing to others. Let this come out of your desire to please the Lord. Don't set up any organization that gets more financial or material supports from the general public, when it isn't a profit-making organization. NGOs and so-called public spirited bodies that do this are not giving anything out but are taking large sums from unsuspecting international donor agencies. They give so little, and take so much. Therefore your decision to give must be wholeheartedly made and induced from above.

You've been blessed in business as a Christian. Right now, your blessing must get others off the grounds of stagnation and poverty, to the glory of God; Gen 12: 1-3. They must feel your help and be lifted; enabled, promoted and delivered by your testimonies. Just talking about people that are suffering, and shuddering in pains or hurts, isn't enough. Reach out to them and bless them; James 2: 15-16; *"If a brother or sister be naked, and destitute of daily food, and one of you say unto them, depart in peace, be ye warmed and filled; notwithstanding ye give them not those things which are needful to the body; what doth it profit?"*

You must help them through your wealth, by taking far-reaching decisions to positively impact them with life-changing helps. You must sow in the life of others. You must sow into the gospel, ministry, training and mission. You must indulge in partnerships, in order to bring God's word to the doorsteps of a perishing world. If you dig your wells, you will do this without permission. To seek the permission of an uncooperative weak-link is to break the flow of spiritual power that God wants to demonstrate.

Prayer
O Lord my God, weed out all tares from my business. Let as many as are opposed to my lifting in business, faith and wellbeing, fall under my feet, in the name of Jesus! Amen!
Further Study
Judges 16:15-21, Isa 29: 18-21

24th Sunday
"Lest there be any fornicator or profane person, as Esau, who for one morsel of meat sold his birthright."
Heb 12: 16
Birth right

Your being a proficient and successful business man is your birth right, take it. It is yours for the asking; Matt 7: 7. Everything is yours. You have been elected, anointed and created to dazzle your generation with the uncommon ingenuity in business, stay blessed! Don't soil your garments, and ruin your excellent calling, ability to meditate gifts of righteousness and holiness, or any beautiful spiritual lifestyle that you already have by becoming profane.

Get to know Jesus more and more and root out negative, immoral and foul relationship out of your heart. Flee from fornication; 1 Cor. 6: 18; *"Flee fornication. Every sin that a man doeth is without the body; but he that commiteth fornication sinneth against his own body."* Flee from adultery; 2 Pet 2: 14; *"Having eyes full of adultery, and that cannot cease from sin; beguiling unsable souls; an heart they have excercised with covetous practices; cursed children."* Flee from idolatry; 1 Jon 5: 21; *"Little children keep yourself from idols."*

Be a moral instructor. Root profanity out of your tabernacles. Don't sell the birth right. It will ruin your business. Take your entitlements of business success by force and stay on top. Hallelujah!

A great musician composed a hit-track that dazzled his producer. While waxing the song, his producer felt the song would be an international hit, and decided to convince him to sell it. He knew the musician was desperate to get money, and decided to tap into that fatal weakness. He therefore called the musician.
"Sir, I don't know if you would like to sell this song?" He asked, as soon as the musician sat down.
"Yea, if I get a buyer!" The Musician said heartily.
"I can get a buyer straightaway!"

"For how much do you think the buyer will take it?"

"Will you take 50, 000 Naira?" The producer offered.

"Give me, 55, 000 Naira, the musician demanded, anxiously. He was broke and needed money to fix some needs.

"Ok, I will give you just that then!" The producer offered and he left.

The producer went to his bankers and secured a little loan for 55, 000 Naira and gave him the money. The musician was very happy and thanked the producer. The producer then took the song to the social media, and shot a video of it. He began to play it in the air waves. He borrowed about 40, 000 naira from friends, and promoted the music for six months. One morning, he got a call from a marketer of African music in London.

"Yea, Am I on to Mr. Silver?" The marketer asked.

"Yea! Mr. Silver is on the line!"

"I'd really like your song, and want to buy it!"

"Ok! How much do you want to buy it?"

"One Million naira? I'll give one Million for it!"

"No! Two Million, sir!"

"Will that go with the video?"

"Yea! It will go with the video!"

"Ok. I'll send my agents then.

The next day his agents met him and paid for the song. The producer got it right, when he promoted the music; expanded his market, and sold it for a higher sum. While the musician was profane. Don't do this!

Prayer line

Father Lord, your word says, I will be head and not the tail; therefore bless me and cause me to surpass the splendour of King Solomon. This year, as I take my place in the Kingdom, open my horizon that I make break forth, breakeven and breakthrough to my next levels in Jesus name! Amen!

Further Study
Ex 23: 26, Deut 19: 14

25th Monday

"And then shall appear the sign of the Son of Man in heaven: and then shall all the tribes of the earth mourn, and they shall see the Son of man coming in the clouds of heaven with power and great glory."

Matt 24: 30

Indescribable glory

I want you to know that your glory is as yet, still indescribable. Glory is when we ascribe power to God. But your glory is when God ascribes His power to you! If you believe in Jesus, the Lord will give you the glory of His father; Jon 17: 22; *"And the glory which thou gavest me I have given them; that they maybe one, even as we are one."*

It is when God reveals His person; awesome nature, His divine and powerful presence that elicits our dependency, humbleness of heart, commitment and the desire to be subject to Him. It is this that brings His glory upon us. When we ascribe power, beauty and excellent knowledge, wisdom and might to God. That's when we invoke His glory on us, and enter His presence with confidence and boldness. It is fashionable to do this, when we fully become believers and are certain that God is controlling our lives. We become certain of God's glory when God demonstrates His purpose in our lives and we have an undying conviction to win souls; Act 1: 8.

In Ex 23; 23- 27, God gave insight into the benefits of been endowed with His glory. *"For mine angel will go before thee, and bring thee in unto the Amorites, and the Hittites, and the Perizzites, and the Canaanites, the Hivites, and the Jubisites: and I will cut them off."* In other to stimulate this attainment of your glory, God expects that you are different from those that He dispossessed from their heritage because of you. Look at Ex 23: 24; *"Thou shalt not bow down to their gods, nor serve them, nor do after their works: but thou shalt utterly overthrow them, and quite break down their images."* The glory is further invoked through a holy, consummate service to God that's deep, compelling and total. Ex 23: 25-26; *"And ye shall serve the LORD your God, and he shall bless thy bread, and thy water; and I will take sickness away from the midst of thee. There shall nothing cast their young, nor be barren, in thy land: the number of thy days I will fulfill."*

Your current business proposals or business plan for the next decade must be channeled to God in prayer, because God is ready to bring them to pass. He has chosen your heart desire, as what will replace the current scheme of things in the business world! You will stand tall and take the front seat in the new scheme of things. If you quit your current level of spiritual ineptitude and weak faith; the things you see right now will vanish and you will be made to head the order of things, under God's command. Joseph had it that way! Now it is your turn. I command the things that are giving you headaches in your business, be brought to naught by the things you desire most in the name of Jesus!

Therefore you must press forward towards the mark of God's glory that's in Christ; Phil 3: 9. If you do, your contemporaries and those competing with you won't be able to look at your face. If they can't look at your face then your files, requests, contracts, deals, meetings and business proposals, will sail through; 2 Cor. 3: 7-11. As a Master-builder and business chieftain, your decision is what counts. You can't afford to fail. I want you to seize Paul's confidence and make it your own; 1 Cor. 3: 10- 15.

Prayer line

O Lord, my God; just as you changed the countenance of Moses that no one could look steadily at his face; imprint my face with your glory, so that what ever pertains to my business, family and finances, may get speedy approvals, support and empowerment in Jesus name! Amen!

Scriptural Study

Ish 42: 1-4, Ps 89: 15-36

26th Tuesday

"I must work the works of him that sent me, while it is day: the night cometh, when no man can work."

John 9: 4

Time and business

Right now, you must understand that your business, life-time or active days of sound physical strength, are timed by the Almighty. Please, don't idle away your time. There will be a time when you won't be able to do any work and would have to depend on what you've done so far. So, why waste your time on frivolities? Go to God; withdraw into your inner sanctum, and stay in God's presence. His presence changes destinies, sustains the cruel fear of old age, and provides needed breakthroughs from seemly dreaded areas, where challenges are toughest. He provides breakthroughs where businesses are riskiest. Therefore stay in God's presence, until His glory robs off on you and your face becomes radiant that men can't withstand you.

Moses had such experience in Ex 34: 35; *"And the children of Israel saw the face of Moses, that the skin of Moses face shone; and Moses put the veil upon his face again, until he went in to speak with him."* When we do this we won't labour to be rich; Pro 23: 4. The lines will fall on us in pleasant places. The Lord Jesus concentrated on his father's business by being conscious of time. He loathed distractions and often took stock of His daily achievements; whether any impact has been made, how men regarded Him and whether the business of the Kingdom was growing; Matt 16: 13-19. He knew how to stay out of trouble and how to handle delicate trouble-makers like the Pharisees and Sadducees. He knew what may create distractions and often avoided them. In Matt 5: 25, He submitted a time-saving blue-print of His ministry that can enhance your business plan and services; *"Agree with thine adversary quickly whiles thou art in the way with him; lest at any time the adversary deliver thee to the judge, and the judge deliver thee to the officer, and thou be cast into prison. Verily I say unto thee thou shalt by no means come out thence till thou hast paid the uttermost farthing."*

Prayer line

Father Lord, deliver me from presumptuous sins that I may live throughout today in absolute holiness. I receive the mystery of divine commitment and the grace to utilize my time graciously. Help me to eliminate mistakes from my business schedules that I may enjoy your timely interventions at all times, in the name of Jesus! Amen!

Further Study
James 3: 1-2, Matt 13: 17

27th Wednesday

"Then Jesus said unto them, Yet a little while is the light with you. Walk while ye have the light, lest darkness come upon you: for he that walketh in darkness knoweth not whither he goeth."

Jon 12: 35

Elements of time

As a businessman, get hard on time. Don't waste your time. Time yourself and stick to time! Get acquainted with some elements of time. Firstly, time is not measured in terms of seconds, minutes, hours or days, when we are in the Lord. It is measured by how connected we are to God; Ps 90: 4; *"For a thousand years in thy sight are but as yesterday when it is past, and as a watch in the night."* How long, you can stay connected, determines your time in your life. Time is the burden of expressing the divine person. If it took fifty years to become sanctified believer in the Lord Jesus, so that you are able to express Him in the Spirit that's when your time began to run.

Secondly, your time is the weight of your achievements in a chosen field; business, personal dreams, or prizes received from excellence, public acclaim or other laurels garnered, as recognition of your especial ingenuity, in your quest for greatness and success. This is why Paul said all his achievements before he knew the Lord Jesus Christ, are a waste of time; his time began to count, when he knew the Lord Jesus Christ, and pushed his way into divine relevance; Phil 3: 8, *"Yea doubtless, and I count all things but loss for the Excellency of the knowledge of Christ Jesus my Lord: for whom I have suffered the loss of all things, and do count them but dung, that I may win Christ."*

Your time is the decree of success accruable to you as a child of God, who has been duly called and commissioned to work in the Lord's vineyard. Your time is your success ratings in business. You've wasted your time when you have nothing to show as your accomplishments. The Lord defined time in the context of His divine task; Mk 1: 38; *"And he said unto them, Let us go into the next towns that I may preach there also: for therefore came I forth."* We are enjoined by God, to spend all our time in obedience to him; Ps 1: 3, Lk 12: 42-48. Child of God; think about your time right now, and plan how to spend it in the Lord's vineyard; 1 Cor. 3: 13-15; *"Every man's work shall be made manifest: for the day shall declare it, because it shall be revealed by fire; and the fire shall try every man's work of what sort it is. If any man's work abide which he hath built upon, he shall receive a reward. If any man's work shall be burned, he shall suffer loss: but he himself shall be saved; yet so by fire."*

Prayer line

Father Lord, I receive power to use my time judiciously. I receive power to achieve my targets in business; while working in your vineyard in the Jesus name! Amen!

Scriptural Study
Eccl: 13:1-8, Ps: 27: 1-14

28th Thursday

"But they that wait upon the LORD shall renew their strength; they shall mount up with wings as eagles; they shall run, and not be weary; and they shall walk, and not faint."

Ish 40: 31

The balm of waiting

Long ago, I watched a documentary on the giant eagle of the Amazon, and found striking correlations with the way the Lord Jesus expects believers to assert themselves in life, business and ministry, after they are born again; in order to understand the mysteries of their salvation. In the documentary, the mother eagle built a huge nest that was made of fresh branches of tall trees on one of the tallest trees in the dense forest. It laid two eggs on the nest and began sitting on them. She sat on them for some time and hatched them.

Two weeks later they were hatched, a brief competition ensued between the two chicks. One chick that appeared bigger and stronger began to push the other chick out of the nest in the full glare of her mother eagle. Because of nights of humid winds and days of intense heat, the weak chick grew weaker. Then the stronger chick devised another strategy; to starve the weak chick of food and push her out of the mother eagle's care, altogether. Despite her murderous plot the mother eagle refused to intervene. She needed one chick and the most fit of the two!

After awhile, haven been starved for a week, the weak chick died. The mother eagle didn't bother about her gruesome fate but promptly threw her body out of the nest, and lavished her attention on the surviving chick. After three months, she also devised a new strategy. It was time to wean her surviving chick, so she could be separate from her forever. In order to launch her weaning programme, she killed a sloth, tore it to shreds with its razor sharp beak and claws, and fed her surviving chick for the last time. By now the chick was grown, but still too lazy and feeling terribly dependent on her mother.

Two days later, the mother eagle flew out of the nest and didn't bother to return. Her surviving chick was terrified. She waited, wailed and cried for her mother to return, but didn't see her. She didn't know her mother wanted her to shed her excess weight, become independent and resume her life-long art of hunting prey. Faced with the possibility of starvation, the grown chick began to flap her wings. She hopped on branches of the huge tree but couldn't bring herself to fly. Two days later, she became more determined to fly. She flapped her wings and leapt upwards. As soon as her flying instincts became stronger, she flew out of her nest with a screeching cry. She exercised the right of an adult eagle and soared into the sky.

Because you are established in the Lord Jesus, you know all things; Col 2:3; *"In whom are hid all the treasures of wisdom and knowledge."* You know where you belong, in order to become established in business. The Lord will bring an assortment of his financial blessings your way that will astound you soon. You won't be moved or threatened by the instability, or powerlessness that often assail other businessmen, because you have a comforter that's sent to you by God, to cushion such challenges; Col 2: 2; *"That their hearts might be comforted, being knit together in love, and unto all riches of the full assurance of understanding, to the acknowledgement of the mystery of God, and of the father, and of Christ.* Paul said we must bear fruits; Gal 5: 22-26. As soon as the embattled eaglet knew she could flap her heavy wings, she had hopped out of the nest; flopped and flew away!

Prayer line

Father Lord, I receive the power, special gifts of perseverance, knowledge, wisdom and divine insight, in order to overcome my challenges in business. I thank you for your salvation; next-levels and double-portions. I break stagnation, hardship and financial predicament in the name of Jesus! Amen!

Scriptural Study
Josh 3:10, Judges 16: 28-29

29th Friday

"They shall take up serpents; and if they drink any deadly thing, it shall not hurt them; they shall lay hands on the sick, and they shall recover."

Mk 16: 18

The missing link

A link is a chain of events that explains some logic; a sequence of facts that offers explanation to a phenomenon. There are missing links in spiritual matters that shouldn't disturb your faith. In fact your faith is designed to bridge any missing link in your understanding of the word of God. Don't be bothered by any missing link today as you stay in God's presence. The Lord will reveal the links, no matter how disturbing or mysterious the links are.

In Num 11:6-8; God explained His relationship with those in the Spirit. *"And he said, hear now my words: if there be a prophet among you, I the LORD will make myself known unto him in a vision, and will speak unto him in a dream. My servant Moses is not so, who is faithful in all mine house. With him will I speak mouth to mouth, even apparently, and not in dark speeches; and the similitude of the LORD shall he behold: wherefore then were ye not afraid to speak against my servant Moses?"*

Links are supplied by visions, dreams, expert use of wisdom and revelation. You don't read the scriptures to find missing links. You must be elected to find them. Stubborn links are personally handled by the Lord; Eph 1: 17; *"That the God of our Lord Jesus Christ, the Father of glory, may give unto you the spirit of wisdom and revelation in the knowledge of him."* As soon as the Lord decides to reveal the links, he will give the Spirit of Wisdom and Revelation in the Knowledge of him, and everything you want to know will fall in place; Matt 10: 26; *"Fear them not therefore: for there is nothing covered, that shall not be revealed; and hid, that shall not be known."*

A friend walked up to me and said he had a pressing question to ask me.

"Go ahead and ask it." I said.

"Ok you say Jesus is the Son of God; is God married?"

I laughed and told him, you don't ask such questions. That's a missing link. Your mind can't fathom the answer that I will give because you're carnally minded."

"I've another question." He said triumphantly.

"Ok, I'm ready, ask."

"Who created God?"

"That again is a missing link. When you're born again, you will know. When you are in the Spirit you don't ask such questions."

The Lord will teach you and bring you safely to where you can enjoy your blessing. Don't bother yourself about how the Lord will do it; Phil 1: 6; *"Being confident of this very thing, that he which hath begun a good work in you will perform it until the day of Jesus Christ."* Jesus taught that the power of the kingdom is such that it grows, expands and nourishes you, and you don't know how. It is like a mustard seed that will soon become grown and shelter birds of every kind. From little beginning, you will become a mighty business man, having treasured empires of chain of blue-chip businesses.

Prayer

Father Lord, guide me on my way to the truth; keep me in your presence all the time. Lead me in the way of Holiness, Righteousness and Joy, in the Holy Spirit. Cause me to partake in your glory, in the name of Jesus! Amen!

Scriptural Study

Acts 12:1-18, 1 Cor. 1: 19-23

30st Saturday

"I waited patiently for the LORD; and he inclined unto me, and heard my cry."

Ps 40: 1

Impatience

Because of the pressure of life, especially when we expect too much from the world and are idle; doing nothing, we are forced to become hasty, easily worried and not prepared to 'waste further time,' because we think 'time waits for no one.' God's approach to such belief, after we've been called or born again, is break our speed, so we can concentrate on Him and master our path of success. The best place for this, and that's how the Lord sees you, is to serve time in some prison facility, (this could be spiritual or physical) where you lose your liberty, are constrained to suffer indignities, are dependent on the goodwill of others, or where the pressure to be free from the trap of stagnation becomes excruciating, suffocating and burdensome. This is what God uses to shape the destinies of His children.

God can bless you when He makes you to know the forces that shape the destinies of men. He does this so you can reinvent the trend of your family history, or discover and takeover the hidden treasures of darkness. He exposes you to the pestilent elements, the hidden forces of creation, secrets of defunct empires and pool of wealth in the Spirit realm, from where you're made to tap them and become a master of your times. In order to do this, He chastises you by making you to pass through the forge of affliction, discipline you with the mystery pain, mental repression and physical oppression, so you can fully acquire what is required to have inner strengths, endurable will and a granite character, knowledge or skill that none can surpass or challenge. He uses the tool of pressure, lack or affliction, to expand the hearts and souls of his chosen vessels.

In order to do this, God uses idleness to prepare the hearts of the hasty, restless and indolent. He uses courage to strengthen the minds of the fearful; knowledge to refashion and expand the hearts of the ignorant, and boldness to embolden the lives of the chicken-hearted. Examples are many. Take up your cross today, and face the challenges of your business; Matt 10: 38; *"And he that taketh not his cross, and followeth after me, is not worthy of me."* Be patient therefore, take up your cross, and follow Jesus. He will turn your business around and bless you mightily.

Prayer

Father Lord, let me find especial grace to attain great business testimonies this month. Let me accomplish your divine tasks that I may fulfill my target of business profitability and overall family success. Fill me with enduring power, grace, peace and breakthroughs in Jesus name! Amen!

Scriptural Study
Job 1:1-3, Pro 19: 9

31ˢᵗ Sunday
Flee from adversity

"I am the God of Beth-el, where thou anointedst. The pillar, and where thou vowedst a vow unto me: now arise, get thee out from this land, and return unto the land of thy kindred."

We must flee from trouble or appearance of evil and concentrate on our business in order to reap maximum profits; Matt 5: 25-26; *"Agree with thine adversary quickly, whiles thou art in the way with him; lest at any time the adversary deliver thee to the judge, and the judge deliver thee to the officer, and thou be cast into prison. Verily I say unto thee, thou shalt by no means come out thence, till thou hast paid the uttermost farthing.* Maximum profits go with maximum concentration. No business thrives on half measures. You either give yourself to your business or lose your business.

Jacob was discreet while assessing his business environment; Gen 31: 2; *"And Jacob beheld the countenance of Laban, and behold, it was not toward him as before."* He was disfavoured by the terms of a pro-Laban contract which was nothing but a hire-contract deal; Gen31: 7; *"Your father hath deceived me, and changed my wages ten times: God suffered him not to hurt me."* In other words, Jacob had some business terms with Laban but they were fluid and could be twisted the way Laban liked.

Jacob couldn't resist him; he was at Laban's mercy; Gen 31: 5-6. He understood that any confrontation with Laban would ruin his young family and vast business interests. Laban tied him with his marriage to his two daughters. He further had immense control over him as an elder, uncle, father in-law, and a son of the soil. Besides Jacob had a large family that was still growing; who regarded the foxy and witty Laban, as their grand father. These ties were difficult to break.

The flocks of Jacob were so many that he needed divine insurance to move them over a long distance without being seen. God had blessed him immensely. Despite this wealthy testimony however, he was hamstrung and immobile. Consequently, Laban dealt with Jacob, as if he was his slave. Jacob didn't like it. There was only one way of escape; he had to flee from Laban without telling him. God approved this and Jacob fled; Gen 31: 13. Don't wait until your business is destroyed by vicious fighters; weigh the chances and flee from adversity and retrogression.

Prayer line

Father Lord, give me the grace to tackle any kind of adversity in my business; let your overflowing wisdom and divine peace rule my business continually, until I begin to reap huge business profit in the name of Jesus!

Scriptural Study
James 1: 17; 1 Sam 18: 12

PART 2

Month OfFebruary, 2016

This Month of February, 2016, will bring you divine grace for your super, bumper breakthroughs that will keep you thrilled throughout the rest of the year. It's your new month of boundless liberty in your career, business and ministry. Don't get worldly business squeeze, melt downs and a tottering economy in your mind. Get on the way of your business profitability by faith, and eschew sharp business practices; Jon 8: 10-11; *"When Jesus had lifted up Himself, and saw none but the woman, he said unto her, Woman, where are thosethine accusers? Hath no man condemned thee? She said, No man, Lord. And Jesus said unto her, Neither do I condemn thee?"*

1ˢᵗMonday

"He that cometh from above is above all: he that is of the earth is earthly, and speaketh of the earth: he that cometh from heaven is above all."

Jon 3: 31

Power from above

The days Moses led the children of Israel out of Egypt, and through the wilderness, remains the toughest, trying and most anxious moment inhuman history; Ex 14: 30; *"Thus the LORD saved Israel that day out of the hand of the Egyptians: and the people feared the LORD, and believed the LORD, and his servant Moses."* A group of former slaves, numbering a little more than a million, marched into freedom through an unknown territory. There were high expectations.

The Israelites hungered for freedom. God sought to have them onto Himself; an exclusive nation of priests and kings. Moses' role was to reconcile these high expectations. The children of Israel thirsted, hungered and yearned, to snatch more promises of hope, goodwill, security and quest for survival that God and Moses kindled. Being pressed to fight for their survival and ultimate fulfillment of God's promises, they faced terrible odds from ferocious enemies, which made their dependence on God inevitable. God desired to fulfill his 400 years old promise to Abraham His friend. This desire made God to plague Egypt with plagues, and unleashed divine power from above, to direct their paths; Ex 14: 18; *"And the Egyptians shall know that I am the LORD, when I have gotten me honour upon Pharaoh, upon his chariots, and upon his horsemen."*

Look upward today, and ask God to invest you with His divine power;; Acts 2: 1-4.Peter who was once frightened, and openly disowned the Lord Jesus, suddenly became the spokesman of the disciples on the day of Pentecost. He stood his grounds in a dangerous territory that was full of unbelievers and boldly addressed the Sanhedrin; Acts 4: 13, *"Now when they saw the boldness of Peter and John, and perceived that they were unlearned and ignorant men, they marveled; and they took knowledge of them, that they had been with Jesus."*

Prayer line

Father Lord, bless me beyond my widest dreams this new month of 2016; cause my cup of glory to overflow with your blessings. Surprise me with your eternal love, mercy and divine protection; heal me O Lord, in Jesus name! Amen!

Further Study
Gal 2: 14, Eph 4: 22-24

2ndTuesday

"The wicked walk on every side when the vilest men are exalted."

Ps 12: 8

Perfectionists

Resent perfectionism and don't be a perfectionist. Live by faith and rejoice in your salvation. The righteous shall live by faith and win the battles of life. God wanted Joseph to believe in Him and know that He alone will fulfill his dreams. God loathes perfectionists. People, who think they don't need God; that look at things judgmentally and think they know more than others. Fault finders, rabble rousers and critics.

He dislikes self-taught thinkers and self-centered geniuses that don't need His grace, power nor hungers for His glory. God loath men like Nebuchadnezzar, who beats their chests, and say what they have achieved. The times of such men doesn't last. Be patient and wait upon the Lord. He will make you to be remembered forever. He will brand you for everlasting greatness. Don't take risky steps that will ruin your business and destiny. If you are led by the Lord Jesus, you will see where He is taking you. When we think we know it all we throw caution to the winds and ruin our business expectations.

Despite the fact that Joseph prospered in Portipher's house, God wanted him to be ruler of Egypt. Portipher's house was a narrow, restrictive dream. It had no world outlook and was useless under the circumstances God sought to create in Israel. In Portipher's house he was still be a slave but as an Egyptian statesman, he will be Lord and master of Egypt. God decided to purify, strengthen and equip Joseph for this glorious path that He chose for him.

His choice was the instrument of prison life; a baptism of suffering; Ps 105: 17-21; *"He sent a man before them, even Joseph, who was sold for a servant: whose feet they hurt with fetters: he was laid in iron, until the time that his word came: the word of the Lord tried him. The king sent and loosed him; even the ruler of the people, and let him go free. He made him Lord of his house, and ruler of all his substance."*

From Portipher's home, God brought Joseph into the limelight of Egyptian statesmanship. He made him Lord of Pharaoh's house and ruler of Egypt. Before this, Joseph attempted to break his divine trial. He showed signs of impatience but the Lord ignored him, until he realized the entire plan was from God; Gen 40: 14; *"But think on me when it shall be well with thee, and show kindness, I pray thee, unto me, and make mention of me unto pharaoh, and bring me out of this house."*

Prayer line

Father Lord; lead me to the Rock that is greater than I, that I may see all your goodness in the land of the living. Change my life with your glorious power, and cause me to experience true and lasting greatness in my spiritual, business and ministerial life, in Jesus name! Amen!

Scriptural Study
Col 2: 8-19, 1 Cor. 8: 9

3rd Wednesday

"And when he had spent all, there arose a mighty famine in that land; and he began to be in want."

Lk 15: 14

Lost time

Your lost time in life, business and spiritual duties to the Lord, is when you fail to do what you ought to do, in order to be sure of God's eternal mercy, faithfulness and peace. When you neglect your gifts, you truncate your time; 1 Tim 4: 14; *"Neglect not the gift that is in thee, which was given thee by prophecy, with the laying on of the hands of the presbytery.*"What you need in order to receive God's goodwill in your life, business and ministry, is a full engagement in the kingdom.

Lost time is when you aren't faithful, dutiful; or reliable in your calling to win souls for the Lord Jesus. When you neglect to expand the frontiers of the Kingdom of God, or live an inspiring Christian life that ought to be a testimony for channeling the Lord's blessings into the lives of others, you've both lost and wasted your time. Paul, while writing on his Christian life, wrote about his times in 2 Tim 4: 7; *"I have fought a good fight, I have finished my course, I have kept the faith."*

He looked back at his life and found that he had done well. From the day he was converted to preach the kingdom, to when he declared in 1 Tim 6: 12, where he counseled believers to fight the good fight; Paul gave a good account of himself as a great evangelist, church-builder, preacher, writer and leader. He spurned riches and pursued a path of God's glory, holiness and righteousness with unmatched vigour; 1 Tim 6: 9-10; insisting that the love of money is the root of all evil. Paul understood the glory of Christ in a manner that astounded his contemporaries; 1 Tim 6: 13-15; *"I give thee charge in the sight of God, who quickeneth all things, and before Christ Jesus, who before Pontius Pilate witnessed a good confession; That thou keep this commandment without spot, unrebukable, until the appearing of our lord Jesus Christ: which in his times he shall show, who is the blessed and only potentate, the King of kings, and Lord of lords."*

Paul didn't lay claim to extra-ordinary status, but had in abject meekness and unrivaled humility, deposed to his being tempted or had been tempted; Gal 4: 13-15. Paul had it rough too. He made countless defenses and suffered betrayals and condemnation. Despite this he fought a good fight and won. That's how we ought to be in ministry and business.

We understand in Phil 3: 4-5 that Paul was a man 'who had no confidence in the flesh.' He never tried to lay claim to his high pedigree and veer away Christ. When people think of their backgrounds they become proud and waste time in frivolities. Like Moses he sacrificed his opportunities, rewards and physical glory for his ministry. In other words, in the course of his calling, Paul didn't waste time on garnishing his background and taking about his legal fame, popularity or having powerful connections among the high and mighty. In numerous writings, he castigated his bad reputation as a persecutor and prosecutor of the Church.

Paul knew that what he needed in life was Christ and held on to Him, to the end. He understood peculiar challenges and resolved them. He fought gallantly, and won both physical and spiritual battles. We lose time, when we have no proof of having fought the good fight and have a deep yearning in our hearts that we haven't really lived well. We lose time when we don't know the battlefield and how to fight the good faith of faith. Don't waste your time today, for what truly count is the time we spent on the Lord's work and not our quest for any form of unearned glory.

We lose time when we lose our will to serve God. In such fatal loss of will, zeal and satisfaction, there is a sad and continuing proof of having lived our lives in gross disobedience to God. Haven failed to stay in the Lord's presence in order to get acquainted with His will and be under His divine leading. We suffer loss of time, when we could have made profound sacrifices that would've changed our businesses, spiritual lives and financial fortunes; have great faith and be armed with the power to change our current predicament or perform important covenant duties in order to merit a better and more stable future that's seeped in God's love, peace and increase.

Prayer line

Father Lord, cause me to regain all my lost years; the years that the locust took from me that I maybe great and know you are the Lord of times and seasons in the name of Jesus! Amen!

Further Study
James 2: 19, 1Jon 3: 10

4ᵗʰ Thursday

"He staggered not at the promise of God through unbelief; but was strong in faith, giving glory to God."

Rom 4: 20

Fortify your inheritance

A friend told me thesad story of his polygamous family that often made him miserable each time he thought of getting married. His father was a wealthy business man, who soldPeugeot automobiles in the 80s. He later established a brewery, and other numerous businesses that thrived as late as 2005, when his estate devolved on his children. He wasn't a Christian, and married many wives. His wives in turn had many children. As the children grew, the tension surrounding his vast family estate became noticeable. Cracks began to appear.

The first wife, Mrs. G, had eighth children that were all females. The second wife had five children that were all males. His third wife had two males. His last wife had three females. Being the first wife and the one with grown up female children, Mrs. G wasn't a happy woman. She plotted how she could inherit her husband's properties, even if there was a customary practice that females don't inherit the estates of their late fathers. Mrs. G decided that the best way to transfer her husband's properties to her female children, would be to empower them, so they could inherit their father's estates, irrespective of the customary practice at the time. She knew if she fortified their rights, there will be a way to undo the customary law or practice. She put her acts together, and trained her eldest daughter as a Lawyer. Her eldest daughter was very successful in legal practice and married an activist who became the Executive Governor of her state. Mrs. G trained her second daughter, as a military officer. She was a Major in the Army, at the time her father died. Mrs. G trained her third daughter as a pilot; the first in the country. Her fourth and fifth children were outstanding bankers. The sixth, seventh and eighth, were trained as police officers.

When they became old enough to marry, Mrs. G gave her daughters to wealthy suitors. The young men were mostly the illustrious sons of her family friends that were very rich and influential. This move by Mrs. G further fortified the position of her daughters and invoked fear around her. My friend was born out of wedlock. Even though he was his father's eldest son, and supposed heir under customary law. Despite this, his half-sisters, being fully advantaged and very successful, banished him from ever entering his father's estate. He managed to train himself as a nurse, and had a little chemist shop opposite his father's compound. His attempt to be united with his late father failed each time he tried to see him.

When his father died, the elders of his family asked him to move to his father's compound, as was the custom but the daughters of Mrs. G, especially her daughter that was a Major, and who was more daring than others, barred him from his father's compound. They threatened him, arrested him several times, and denied him his inheritance under customary law because he didn't do enough to fortify his inheritance. Being the eldest son of a wealthy man, isn't enough, you must do what will guarantee your inheritance. My friend had no legal means to pursue his rights in court and couldn't stand the threats of the children of Mrs. G. After many years, the elders of his family advised him to withdraw his claim to his father's estate.

Prayer line

Father Lord, I refuse to be counted as a failure in business, family and ministry in this generation. Grant me a prosperous and long life; bless my investments, my business prospects, and overall family life, in the name of Jesus! Amen!

Further Study

Gal 5: 16, Jon 16: 15

5th Friday

"And not only so, but we glory in tribulations also: knowing that tribulation worketh patience; and patience, experience; and experience, hope..."

Rom 5: 3-4

Build on experience

Knowledge is power, but experience is golden. Don't only seek men with unique knowledge in your area of business but also seek men with experience. Because we are inexperienced we often let clear-cut opportunities slip out of our grip. After King Solomon ruined his relationship with

God, by marrying strange women that turned his heart away from God, God vowed to snatch the kingdom from his son; 1 Kings 11:29-39.He would divide the kingdom in two, and leave half, the tribe of Judah to David, for his outstanding spiritual successes and because of God's promise to leave him a line of Kings in Jerusalem. As soon as King Solomon died, and his arch-criticand former minister, Jeroboam the son of Nebat, returned from exile, he gathered the opposition to ask Rehoboam, who was King Solomon's son to ask for a major policy change that will ease their burdens.

For King Rehoboam to become King, he was faced with the request of the opposition in Tirzah. All Israelites expected a new regime that will allow them some respite, haven built numerous projects like the temple, the King's breathtaking palaces, several castles, and stately mansions, private estates of his trusted aides, new cities, the wall of Jerusalem, and other vast kingdom infrastructure to the detriment of their individual lives. Many believed because King Solomon was from Judah, he concentrated all the benefits of his projects in Judah. Besides King Solomon indulged in needless ostentation, had a vast family, friends and diplomatic offices that pursued annoying, ostentatious lifestyles that reduced the average Israelite to rags, as they were required to pay heavy taxes while they lived in penury.

Rather than go to God in prayers, and seek his face, or at least consult and do what the counselors of his late father advised him, King Rehoboam made the ancient mistake of starters, and decided to obey the silly counsel of his fellows, known as young men, who in all probability, were born and bred in luxury, inherited huge resources from vast family wealth and had no experience, nor insight into how others felt; 1 Kings 12: 10; *"And the young men that were grown up with him spake unto him, saying, thus shalt thou speak unto this people that spake unto thee, saying, thy father made our yoke heavy but make thou it lighter unto us; thus shalt thou say unto them, my little finger shall be thicker than my father's loins. And now whereas my father did lade you with a heavy yoke, I will add to your yoke; my father hath chastised you with whips, but I will chastise you with scorpions."*

Prayer line

Father Lord; connect me to your glorious throne of grace that I maybe worthy of your divine wisdom, eternal knowledge and glory. Take me where I can receive your divine help, support and mercy in the name of Jesus! Amen!

Further Study

Job 5: 12, Ps 29: 2

6th Saturday

"And I will make drunk her princes, and her wisemen, her captains, and her rulers, and her mighty men: and they shall sleep a perpetual sleep, and not wake, saith the King, whose name is the LORD of hosts."

Jer. 51: 57

Loss of insight

What's insight? It is the ability to see the deeper perspectives of your business plan, intents of staff or business partners, your growing clientele or circumstances that reflect a leading from God. Ask God for insight; ask Him to restore your lost gifts or ability that you may take center stage in the manifestation of grace, in your life today. Insight is deep knowledge or understanding of something that others consider mysterious. You're at home in the handling of mysteries.

We must be conscious of God's leading, for us to become sure we are indeed blessed. Don't break the thin line of God's spirit that links you to God's power, knowledge, leading or connection, and be eager to renew any snapped connections, as that maybe too costly. We often cut our communication links to God, through sin; even though that is the price we should pay, to remain connected; Matt 13: 15-16; *"For this people's heart is waxed gross, and their ears are dull of hearing, and their eyes they have closed; lest at any time they should see with their eyes, and hear with their ears, and should understand with their heart, and should be converted, and I should heal them. But blessed are your eyes, for they see: and your ears, for they hear."*

Insight is when your eyes and ears are blessed by God; Ps 40: 6; *"Sacrifice and offerings thou didst not desire; mine ears hast thou opened; burnt offering and sin offering hast thou not required.* ?When you can see and evaluate your kingdom roles in bright and clear colours. When you can walk in divine blessings and reassure yourself that the Lord is on the throne. That's when you reap supernatural benefits and comes on top. Insight is when you both see and hear Christ speak to your heart; when you experience strategic leading, for your overall breakthroughs in life. The grace often opens up our hearts, and drives us towards the direction of our blessings.

As soon as he got insight of what to do, Isaac gracefully overcame the devourers that withstood him and quickly regained the glory of his business. He named his business after God, and credited his prosperity, fortune, stability and overall state of fruitfulness, to God. Like the prodigal son, we lose our time and fortune, when we lose insight of who we are, or what we should do, in order to change the course of our misfortune; Lk 15: 18-24. With needed insight, we gain time, make steady advances in God's plan for us, and become startling success in our families, having spiritual wellbeing and business. When we do what Moses did, in

Heb 11: 16-25; when he refused to be called the son of Pharaoh's daughter, but choose rather to suffer affliction with the people of God, than enjoy the pleasures of sin for a season; we become a staggering success in God's plan.

Prayer line

Father Lord, put me in your presence daily, because in your presence there is fullness of joy, and the power of your blessings are forever more; cause the lines of your glory to fall onto me in pleasant places in the name of Jesus! Amen!

Scriptural Study
Ish 36: 1-22, Dan 4: 4-27

7th Sunday

"Or else how can one enter into a strong man's house, and spoil his goods, except he first bind the strong man? And then he will spoil his house."

Matt 12: 29

Invention

Invention is what you need to bind the strongman of competition, challenge, poverty or recurrent misfortune in business. Look up to God for a new way of doing your business that will confound your contemporaries. To bind something is to do what will discomfit and utterly overwhelmit. It is often the last resort in other to overwhelm your enemies or hostile business environments. Invention is a swift move that paralyses the forces of retrogression, when we have been assured of God's divine direction!As a Christian businessman, learn to acquire skills, experience and knowledge that can you go with the times and create a new way of doing things!

An invention supported by God is what will help you stay long in business, and rake in supernormal profits; gain control over the future, pursue the projected fortune of your business and dream of endless profits. Invention will take your competitors by surprise, bring them to their knees and stifle the voice of any opposition in your area of interests. Just as worldly businessmen spend billions of dollars in research efforts, so as to invent something that will give them an upper hand in business, you must go to God by faith, and let him put something in your heart that will change your dwindling fortunes in business.

God did it for Jacob, when he faced a hard business environment in the home of Laban; Gen 31: 8; *"If he said thus, The speckled shall be thy wages; then all the cattle bare speckled: and if he said thus, The rings raked shall be thy hire; then bare all the cattle rings raked. Thus God hath taken away the cattle of your father, and given them to me."* We are forced to invent something when we are faced with a challenge that has become some crisis if drastic action isn't taken to curb it. The example of David offers the characteristic nature of a Christian invention that can attest to your overall life, strategy and business success; and is a winning strategy for those whose dream is to become great in business.

Prayer line

Father Lord, cause me to receive a special leading today that will break my current state of stagnation in Jesus name! Amen!

Further Study
Pro 13: 4, 2 Chr. 9: 23

8th Monday

"Teach me thy way, O LORD, and lead me in a plain path, because of my enemies."

Ps 27: 10

Necessity and creativity

One day, David was keeping his father's sheep when a lion came and attempted to kill one of them. David fought the lion with all his might and killed it but at great risk. In order not to take such risk in future, he invented a special weapon; a sling that slung stones from a distance, and decided that it was what he would use to defend his sheep. Whenever he was alone, he would practice with the sling. He will kill birds, hares and antelopes. One day, a bear came to attack his sheep, and David killed it with this special invention. He used the sling from a safe distance and killed it in seconds. Rather than stay in the wild and combat lions, tigers and bears with his bare hands, he now had a special weapon with which to defend himself and protect his business. Invent a special weapon with which you can protect your business today. Don't give in despair look up to God. I don't know the particular business that you have. Every business has areas of necessity and space for creativity

When God rejected King Saul and needed to replace him, he sent Samuel to the home of Jesse. Everyone was surprised when God directed Samuel to anoint David as future King of Israel. David had spent years living in the wild. But on this occasion he became a very important person. His elder brothers ran to where he to call him. Where your business is doesn't matter, what matter is whether you are born again and can receive inspired ways of doing things as a businessman. Are you in God's list of great men and women, destined to make it in business?

At the time David was secretly anointed by Samuel, the Philistines who were hostile neighbours of Israel were at war with Israel. Goliath, a Philistine General, and a giant of immense size and experience, came out of the ranks of the Philistine army to challenge Israel; saying King Saul should get him a man that will be bold enough to fight him. If the man killed him, Israel will become the masters of the Philistines but if he kills the man, Israel will serve the Philistines. Many soldiers fled from Goliath each time he came up to challenge Israel. Goliath boasted in this fashion for forty days, until David appeared on the scene, when his father sent him to go and see how his three elder brothers that were in the warfront were faring.

Prayer line

Father Lord; cause me to invent what will cause my business to flourish today, in the name of Jesus. Cause me to go out and find pasture. Touch me and make me became unique in all aspects of my life. I decree that as I go out today, I shall discover the secrets of my business profitability and use it to expand it in Jesus name!

Scriptural Study
Luke 18: 1-8, Jon 7: 14-18

9th Tuesday

"The Lord looked down from heaven upon the children of men, to see if there were any that did understand, and seek God. They are all gone aside, they all together become filthy: there is none that doeth good, no, not one."

Ps 14: 2 & 3

Search

God is searching the earth for a worthy partner with whom He will fulfill His eternal will for mankind. God needs you. Being a businessman or woman like Job, makes you all the more His favorite. God said of Job that there was none like him on the earth and he was right; Job 1: 8; *"And the Lord said unto Satan, Hast thou considered my servant Job, that there is none like him in the earth, a perfect and an upright man, one that feareth God, and escheweth evil?"* Despite his horrible trial of faith and the terrible things he suffered, Job never sinned against God; his end was better than his beginning; Job 42: 10.

In every crisis, learn to stand up and declare your stand to work with God. God searched the earth at a time and found Noah. At another time he found Abraham. He searched for a deliverer and found Moses. He searched again when King Saul failed terribly and found David, saying; Ps 89: 20; *"I have found David my servant; with my holy oil have I anointed him: with whom my hand shall be established: mine arm shall also strengthen him. The enemy shall not exact upon him; nor the son of wickedness afflict him. And I will beat down his foes before his face, and plague them that hate him. "*Today, the Lord is searching and looking for great partners of His will. I want you to fill the need right now. Become the man of the moment. The qualities needed are uprightness, perfection, fear of God and hard work.

The search for faithful workers is on; Jon 4: 35- 38.The moment you are selected by God, your times will be wrapped with indescribable power, fortune and blessings. There are certain decisions you have to make in order to prove your sincerity and need for consideration. In order to meet the great need, Joseph decided not to commit adultery with Portipher's wife, and soon became the greatest man of his generation; Gen 39: 9. David decided not to kill King Saul, when had the opportunity 1 Sam 24: 11.

King Saul died in battle and David became King of Israel. Daniel and his friends, proposed in their hearts not to eat the King's meat, and they excelled as statesmen in Babylon; Dan 1: 8.Even when Nebuchadnezzar put them in a fiery furnace they weren't hurt. A fourth man believed to be Christ appeared in the furnace. Jesus narrowed all you need to do perfection; Matt 5: 48; *"Be ye therefore perfect, even as your Father which is in heaven is perfect. "*What have you proposed not to do as proof of faithfulness, uprightness and perfection?

Prayer line

Father Lord, clothe me with your glory that I may prosper in my business. I reject hindrances, demonic barricades and snail-speed spirit in my business, ministry and calling. Father, revolutionizes me today in the name of Jesus! Amen!

Further Study
Matt 19: 10-12, 1Pet 5:

10th Wednesday

"And he said, who art thou, Lord? And the Lord said, I am Jesus whom thou persecutest: it is hard for thee to kick against the pricks."

Acts 9: 5

Don't oppose your master

I adjure you not to oppose the Lord in any way today, as He is ready to forgive your sins, and reveal Himself to you with compelling power. The Lord is set to show you His signs and wonders. Therefore humble yourself today, and go to Him like a child. The Lord will accept you and bring you into the fold of His saints. Do you feel uncomfortable when you hear the word of God? If you have such problem, confess it and renounce unbelief. You may be suffering from the consequences of ancestral curses unbelief, a special spiritual condition known as 'Pricks.' Pricks could be very dangerous when left untended for long. Pricks are the deep pain we experience when we're told the truth. It started with the High Priest, the day he asked Christ his true spiritual personality; Matt 26: 62-65. Christ told him he was the Son of God and he felt so pained and hurt that he tore his robes. When the High Priest does this, anyone who was the object of his action would die. He therefore pronounced Jesus guilty of blasphemy and sentenced Him to death.

When the Jews heard the revelations of Stephen, they weren't just pricked by it, they rushed upon him, dragged him outside the city, and stoned him to death; Acts 7: 57; *" Then they cried out with a loud voice, and stopped their ears, and ran upon him with one accord, and cast him out of the city, and stoned him: and the witnesses laid down their clothes at a young man's feet whose name was Saul."*

Pricks are spiritual truths that shows we aren't born again, and aren't in the book of life; Jon 3: 18; *"He that believeth on him is not condemned: but he that believeth not is condemned already, because he hath not believed in the name of the only begotten of Son of God.*" Background to the martyrdom of Stephen can be found in Acts 6: 9; *"Then there arose certain of the synagogue, which is called the synagogue of the Libertines, and Cyrenians, and Alexandrians,, and of them of Cilicia and of Asia, disputing with Stephen."*

When men oppose the Lord and are shown their folly, they grow pricks in their hearts and devise ways to side-step their imminent condemnation. That's why pricks are the unconscious resistance we put up against the word of God, because of the certainty of our eternal destruction; Rev 20: 15; *"And whoever was not found written in the book of life was cast into the lake of fire.*" When the siblings of Moses; Aaron and Miriam, challenged his authority as the leader of

Israel, God defended Moses openly, and revealed the reason why He made him to lead Israel; Num 12: 1-9. God told them that Moses was the meekest man in the surface of the earth, for giving up his privileged position, as a prince of Egypt, to become a Shepherd boy in the burning deserts of Sinai. Moses gave up everything; including his pride and privileges. That's what endeared him to God. Moses served as a shepherd boy to Jethro, his father-in-law, for 40 years. He left Egypt at the age of 40, and returned when he was 80!

Because He is looking around for zealous, competent and faithful men like you, he got Paul involved in ministry for his exceeding zeal, notwithstanding his brutality against Christians. His intellectual mentality, deep literariness and creative disposition, endeared him to the Lord, and God decided to reveal Himself to him; Acts 9: 16: *"For I will show him how great things he must suffer for my name's sake."*

Prayer line

Father Lord, reveal yourself to me more and more today that I may serve you all the days of my life in the name of Jesus! Amen!

Scriptural Study
LK 18: 1-8, Jon 7: 14-18

11ᵗʰ Thursday

"Unto Timothy, my own son in the faith: Grace, mercy, and peace, from God our Father and Jesus Christ our Lord."

1 Tim 1: 2

Mentoring

You must acquire relevant skill from a mentor in order to be committed to the doctrine of Christ. Your belief must be cross-checked, studied and supervised by a mentor that would offer great insight, oversight and deep spiritual nurture and grounding. Mentoring is a necessity when you are faced with adversity. Having first- hand experience from those that have grown in ministry, reassures us of competence and spiritual usability. Spiritual life thrives in apprenticeship. It is more of a copy-cat enterprise than a self-taught scheme. You must have a master and a mentor that teaches you strategic kingdom secrets, so you don't depend on a swing of your own understanding in ministry.

No amount of studying the scriptures, fasting and prayer can reveal the practical insights you need in ministry or business. You must be under a strict and suitable master and learn the nitty-gritty of your trade. When I praised my graphic artist for his great skill, he told me how he became proficient in graphic design, as a child.

"My boss, who trained me, was a quick tempered, no nonsense man. Any time he gives me something to do, and I am slow about it; he will give me a heavy knock on my head, and a good thrashing too. There is no amount of graphic design that satisfies him."

"Then how did you become so proficient?" I asked.

"I had no choice. I resume at his shop, as early as 6. 30am each day; long before he comes. I sweeps it; arranges the chairs and tables, and put on the computers. I check the engine oil in the generator, and arrange all printed jobs on the shelves. I will study the old jobs he did the previous day, copy them carefully, and begin to do them. When he comes, he will look perfunctorily at them, and give me more difficult jobs for the day. He knows how long it will take to do each job, and expects you to give a clue to what you're doing every minute! That way, I had no time to even eat!"

It is easy to learn from others, than try to get the vast knowledge of the Kingdom, all alone.Go out today and listen to those already in your field, who are now masters, and acquire salient points that madethem the genius they are. No new insights, without explainable sourceand recognized mastery, can stand in this competitive world. Jesus taught that the disciple is not above his master; Matt 10: 24; *"The disciple is not above his master, nor the servant above his lord."* There is clear need to be dependent on someone; a trusted senior or leader that has proven competence in our area of business.

A kind teacher from whom, we derive undiluted inspiration, passion and virtue. There is absolute need to be under someone; a special guide, who has proven spiritual competence, divine ability or resourcefulness. We need someone who is willing to teach us how to become competent, confident and self-assertive in our area of business or ministry; someone from who we can copy a special gift or learn a special ability.

These are some benefits of mentoring that you may need to know.

- Mentoring emboldens faith, expands deeper truths and spiritual knowledge about the Kingdom of God.
- It units the Church and eliminates false doctrines, teachers and faulty submission about the Kingdom of God.
- It is a super high-way for ventilating spiritual knowledge and finding common grounds.

Prayer line

Father Lord; thank you for nurturing my faith and bringing me to the heights of ministry. Lord, send mentors, helpers and pillars to me that I may fulfill my commission in the name of Jesus! Amen!

Further Study
1 Tim 6: 19-21, Rom 5: 8

12th Friday

"Let as many servants as are under the yoke count their own masters worthy of all honour, that the name of God and his doctrine be not blasphemed."

1 Tim 6: 1

Let your mentor speak

Let your mentor speak through you. Let him thrive through your thoughts, decisions and calculations. Let him inspire deep knowledge in your heart, so you can achieve great acts of faith. It was easy for those who saw or listened to the disciples, to know they were taught by the Lord Jesus, as they exuded great boldness, confidence and profound spiritual power.

Their backgrounds, belief and spiritual motivation were the same; Acts4: 13; *"Now when they saw the boldness of Peter and John, and perceived that they were unlearned and ignorant men, they marveled; and took knowledge of them, that they had been with Jesus.* Let men see you, and know you are a transparent, trustworthy and straightforward Christian businessman. From boardroom meetings, to the executions of your office, let it be seen that you're a saint. Let everyone feel the impact of the Holy Spirit around them, as soon as you appear. Such sincerity, such awesome power is what endears you to mentoring.

When Peter and John addressed the Sanhedrin, they immediately knew where they were coming from. They took note of them and concluded they belonged to the Lord Jesus Christ. They hadn't dogmatic stereotypes of the Pharisaic schools that ruled Israel. This doesn't mean we should be hasty in adopting mentors. Great care must be exercised in such noble decisions considering its impact on our calling and business future.

Men who love scriptural writing, difficult verse forms would find Pauline epistles, a ready choice. Peter warned against such mentoring decisions if we aren't led by God, in 2 Pet 3: 15; inferring that only those who may be confident of reading and understand him, should adopt Paul as their Mentor. *"And account that the longsuffering of our Lord is salvation; even as our beloved brother Paul also according to the wisdom given unto him hath written unto you; as also in all his epistles, speaking in them of these things; in which are some things hard to be understood, which they that are unlearned and unstable wrest, as they do also other scriptures, unto their own destruction."*

The most outstanding demonstration of mentorship, where a mentor lived, spoke and thrived, through the mind of a compliant disciple, is the kingly charge King David gave

Solomon, as soon as he became King, and the manner in which Solomon executed the charge, when he became King. In order to live up to the billing of a disciple, Solomon allowed the voice of David, his father, to rule and dominate his being; his decisions, actions and total outlook; 1 Kings 3: 3; *"And Solomon loved the LORD, walking in the statutes of David his father: only he sacrificed and burnt incense in high places."*

What particular charge do you hold dear in the ministry of great men of God? What do you hold dear in the business skills of an outstanding businessman known to you? What have you done about the charge the Lord Jesus gave to all believers in Matt 28: 19-20?I want you to get a mentor today, and grow in your chosen business or ministry.

Prayer line

Father Lord; I cherish the knowledge of all great men of God that excelled in ministry, and the secrets of those who made it in business. Cause me to acquire the mystery of your fellowship today, even as you grant me understanding to find out witty inventions in name of Jesus! Amen!

Scripture Study
1 Kings 3: 5-15, 2 Chr. 9: 22

13th Saturday

"Take heed unto thyself, and unto the doctrine; continue in them: for in doing this thou shalt both save thyself, and them that hear thee."

1   Tim 4: 16

Blueprint of doctrine

For mentoring to be worthwhile, you must have a complete blue-print of doctrine. For doctrine to be worthwhile, it must conform to the dictates of the Holy Spirit. Doctrine must be a cardinal belief, upon which the effectual ministration of Christ can be effective. Doctrine must elicit the full demonstration of faith, sacrifice, and love, baptism of the Holy Spirit, the gift of eternal life, and the punishment of the ungodly. Doctrine must generate followership, compellability, and convey the power of the mystery of godliness. Doctrine must answer to the deep yearning of believers in whatever ages, and not wear away with time nor become a porous, pretentious practice in need of reforms or be ridiculed. It must withstand time, equip and discipline both mentors and students of the word.

To be accounted a true believer, you must be sensitive to the gale of false doctrines, false teachers and their diabolic effect on the Church; 1 Tim 4: 1 *"Now the Spirit speaketh expressly that in the latter times some shall depart from the faith, giving heed to seducing spirits, and doctrines of devils."* You must discern familiar spirits or spirits of divination, whose specialty are the circulation of false, debilitating doctrines and false power-show that awfully limits, and scuttles the true power of God. Jesus outlined some aspects of false doctrines and teachers in Rev; 2: 12-14; *"And to the angel of the church in Pegamos write; These things saith he which hath the sharp sword with two edges; I know thy works, and where thou dwellest, even where Satan's seat is: and thou holdest fast my name, and hast not denied my faith, even in those days wherein Antipas was my faithful martyr, who was slain among you, where Satan dwelleth. But I have a few things against thee, because thou hast there them that hold the doctrine of Balaam, who taught Balac to cast a stumbling block before the children of Israel, to eat things sacrificed unto idols, and to commit fornication."*

Prayer line

Father Lord, I receive the power to track down and utterly defeat all familiar spirits, seducing spirits and spirits of divination, in my area of ministry, today. I refuse to be deceived by those that have departed from the faith in Jesus name! Amen!

Further Study
Acts 8: 18, Matt 26: 31-32

14th Sunday
Auction

"But ye have an auction from the Holy One, and ye know all things."

1 John 2: 20

Be glad that you have an auction for business and that the holy one has called you into the kingdom to explore it. You can't manifest anything and enjoy doing it unless it is given you from above; Jon 3: 27; *"John answered and said, A man can receive nothing, except it be given him from heaven."* The auction is the expression of the gifts of God, by which we exercise dominion in Kingdom engagements. It is what Jesus gave the seventy, when he sent them to witness on His behalf; Luke 10: 1; *"After these things the LORD appointed other seventy also, and sent them two and two before his face into every city and place, whither he himself would come."* In Matt 10: 1; Christ gave his disciples power against unclean spirits, to cast them out and to heal. *"And when he had called unto him his twelve disciples, he gave them power against unclean spirits, to cast them out, and to heal all manner of sicknesses and all manner of diseases."*

Besides this, there is a promise of power in Acts 1: 8; when we receive the anointing. There is also a promise of deliverance. These promises should endear you to Christ and how to be expert in the use of power. When the disciples received it, Peter and John did outstanding miracles. They grew the church and withstood the Sanhedrin. The primary status that we acquire in the anointing is the power and personality of son ship; Acts 2; 7; *"I will declare the decree; the Lord hath said unto me, thou art my son, this day have I begotten you. Ask of me, and I shall give thee the heathen for thine inheritance, and the uttermost parts of the earth for thy possession."*

Know whatever you need to know about the auction. There is no boundary nor limits to the use and exploitation of the auction. The possibilities of your triumph over difficulties and repeated winning strides are boundless. As soon as you get hold of it; explore and exploit it. For instance, a business that commands tremendous activity should be an orderly, well-planned super-structure that offer immediate financial yields, and creates next-levels at will. Depending on how deeply committed or engrossed you are in business. The overall effect of great financial returns in business, must be real, in order to establish and strengthen your commitment. This is the area where business bears striking similarities with kingdom work or ministry. As a believer, and someone in the ministry, your auction must be strong enough for you to service the soul of your business through Christ; overcome inevitable risks, have a clearer vision of a stable business future, and earn positive commendations from a growing clientele.

Paul taught Timothy, whom he called his son, the secret of ministerial success. 2 Tim 3: 10-11; *"But thou hast fully known my doctrine, manner of life, purpose, faith, longsuffering, charity, patience, persecutions, afflictions, which came unto me at Antioch, at Iconuim, at Lystra; what persecutions I endured: but out of them all the Lord delivered me.* Mentoring must go with a copious copying of the works of Christ. It must reflect the pious understanding of an established and well-known mentor.

Prayer line

Father Lord, cause me to excel in business today; equip me with an auction to do gloriously. I take my place of increase, prosperity and breakthroughs. Thank you Lord for giving me a turn-around in Jesus name! Amen!

Further Study
2   kings 4: 3-4; Matt 10: 8-6

15th Monday

"And the wind bloweth where it listeth, and thou hearest the sound thereof, but canst not tell whence it cometh, and whither it goeth: so is every one that is born of the spirit."

Jon 3: 8

Like the wind

The Holy Spirit spreads and effectively distributes special abilities, graces, gifts and wealth-creation insights, through auctions that are given to build and expand the kingdom. The baptism of the Holy Spirit, is however different from the auction to *function* in a particular ministry or business. The baptism is a foundational kingdom experience, while an auction is a restrictive power to accomplish a particular task.

The auction is the effect of the baptism of the Holy Spirit, when made to operate in a particular area of ministry, gifts or divine ability. It often relates to a specific leading or a discharge of divine duty. The auction is also how the Holy Spirit discharges the gifts, fruits and wisdom of any ministerial office. The auction is the unique function of spiritual and business gifts, modeled to minister the doctrine of Christ. It is designed to create excellence in both business and ministry. It is what makes the believer very functional, exceptional and perfect; an icing on the cake of success.

A major character of the Holy Spirit is that it is the center of divine activity; Gen 1: 2; *"And the earth was without form, and void; and darkness was upon the face of the deep. And spirit of God moved upon the face of the water.*" The Holy Spirit provides regulatory services in the kingdom of God; Jon 16: 13; *"Howbeit when he, the spirit of truth, is come, he will guide you into all truth: for he shall not speak of himself; but whatsoever he shall hear, that shall he speak; and he will show you things to come."*

These regulatory functions enable the Holy Spirit to stabilize those that have him, so they can wait upon the Lord; Isaiah 40: 31; *"But they that wait upon the LORD shall renew their strength; they shall mount up with wings as eagles; they shall run, and not be weary; and they shall walk, and not faint."* His demonstration of power empowers the carrier to do his heart desire and accomplish difficult tasks. Such that Abraham became a man of faith, through the Holy Spirit, Sarah received strength to conceive, the promises were guided into the hands of Jacob and not Esau, and the frustrations of Esau were whittled. Jacob's preferred son, Joseph; became great by it.

The Holy Spirit provides guidance, strength, vision and great accomplishment. You can't have the Holy Spirit and you're idle, calm, silent and threatened. It is a divine force that creates agitation, creativity and restiveness. It announces inevitable changes and provides profound overhaul of any system. You can't have the Holy Spirit and you are half-bred, half-baked or unfit and defeated in business. After it has moved, God speaks, creates and does his will; Gen 1: 3.

Prayer line

Father Lord, beautify me with your precious Holy Spirit. Invest me with the power, gifts and knowledge of the Holy

Spirit. Let your grace supply all that I need that I may excel in business and ministry, in Jesus name! Amen!

Further Study

Matt 7: 7, Matt 5: 46

16th Tuesday

"Looking onto Jesus the author and finisher of our faith; who for the joy that was set before him endured the cross, despising the shame, and is set down at the right hand of the throne of God."

Heb 12: 2

Look onto Jesus

If you look onto Jesus, the author and finisher of your faith; you will experience wonders in business, family life and ministry. Do that today. Cast down the things you see, and build up what you don't see, that you may excel in business. The things you don't see are able to change what you see. Looking onto Jesus is more powerful than paying tithes, or sowing seeds. There are no benefits in tithing, if we turn our backs on Jesus. If we sow seeds and are looking elsewhere, we aren't sincere, and will be seen as transgressors; Gal 2: 18. Your business is the perfect place to look onto Jesus, and change negative trends. In Jon 10: 10; Jesus said; *"The thief cometh not, but for to steal, and to kill, and to destroy. I am come that they might have life, and that they might have it more abundantly. "*

Today, the Lord Jesus is prepared to enrich and expand your business. He is ready to take away the burdens of devourers in your business, and demonstrate His kind heartedness and power of life-giving union between you and him. Today, the Lord Jesus is in the business of raising powerful businesses and businessmen from obscurity, to international standards. You must key into His great programme of divine expansion, manifestation and empowerment. What dose it take for the Lord to change the dwindling fortunes of your business. It is when you take up His yoke, which is very light and begin to do wonders with compelling results!

God can bring the best brains into your business, or suddenly give the intellect of a Bill Gates, to your younger son that you are grooming to take over your business. This is the angle that you should channel your prayers and expectations for the future. So you don't bequeath your hard earned legacies to a numskull. Ask God for an auction that will transform God's vision for your business. Ask God for the power to make wealth. God gave the auction of intelligence, wealth-creation, craftsmanship, ingenuity and creativity, to Bazeelel of the tribe of Judah, and Aholiab of the tribe of Dan; Ex 31: 1-6. In order to build the tabernacle and its sacred furniture without difficulty, he also empowered the duo and other wise-hearted persons in Israel. Remember that it is how you combine your business with the auction that you create wealth. The auction multiplies and blesses your business; Gen 1: 28.

In 1 Tim 4: 14; Paul specifically asked Timothy to tap from the auction 'which was given thee by prophecy, with the laying on of the hands of the presbytery.' Which means the auction is distributable, agreeable and expendable by the leadership of the church; James5: 14. After Joseph was bought by Portipher, his master found that his home, family, businesses and everything under Joseph, prospered. He knew when Joseph came, and traced it to his young Hebrew slave, and handed him his entire estate. That's the auction. As soon as you grow in the Lord and operate in it, be assured that everyone around will go in your direction, and manifest the demonstration of God's will, blessings and beneficence.

Prayer line

Father Lord, bequeath the benefits, gifts and goodwill of the Lord Jesus in my life that I may function under an auction of prosperity in the name of Jesus! Amen!

Further Study
James 5: 11, Acts 4: 12

17th Wednesday

"Divers weights, and divers measures, both of them are alike abomination to the LORD."

Pro 20; 10

The scales

When we become committed to ministry, we automatically know flukes, fraudulent business overtures, and criminal trends in business. We know falsehood from a mile. We discern serpentine tricks of the devil in our area of business. How do we achieve this? By holding an imaginary scale in the spirit, with which we weigh all actions including ours. Develop this spiritual practice today, and you will be at peace.

Success or failure in business is more of our conviction, wisdom and knowledge, than being busy all the time or engrossed in our business or ministerial activity. You must be called, and through maturation of the spirit, attain the reward of you're your calling. Without seeing details of a bogus business proposal, or the entire state of shipped goods, you are expected to know, if the business proposal will work or whether the goods are in commercially viable state or not. Through the Spirit you are expected to know the depth, workability, paucity, inherent dangers, and hidden leakages in an otherwise tight and inevitable deal.

Investing on unviable businesses is the dread of investors. Overcome this dread today, by being committed to the Lord Jesus Christ through the Holy Spirit. Ask the Lord for a leading in this direction, and you will become confident, rake in profits from delicate businesses and be sure of your overall success in business.

Unknown to us, God has a divine scale with which He weighs our actions, life, expectations, decisions and heart-desires, before He either blesses us, or abandons us. When Cain and Abel brought their sacrifices to God, God rejected Cain's sacrifice and accepted that of Abel. Why? God gave His reasons in Gen 4: 7;*"If thou does well, shalt not be accepted? And if thou doest not well, sin lieth at the door. And unto thee shall be his desire, and thou shalt rule over him.* In other words God weights the actions, hearts and overall disposition of men before rewarding them accordingly.

When Abraham became less committed to Him, because of 'the Isaac factor,' God rejected the second fiddle role Abraham relegated Him to play, in the scheme of things. Being a jealous God, God asked Abraham to offer Isaac on a certain mountain he would show him; Gen. 22: 10-13. God weighed Abraham's faith and found he lacked concentration, commitment and divine attention. He was losing his grip over his years of commitment and fellowship. God expects you to discover His rule on judgment, equity and justice, through your spiritual maturation. You are expected as Paul said in 2 Cor. 10: 6, to reward all disobedience after your obedience is fulfilled.

Prayer line

Father Lord, expose and utterly defeat every spirit of deception, confusion, betrayal, fraud and cheating, that satanic powers are trying to introduce in my business. I plead the blood of Jesus over my life, family and business. Cause any devourer that's lurking around my business, to be exposed, destroyed and defeated by the Holy Spirit in Jesus name! Amen!

Further Study
Gen 3: 1-6, Matt 13: 19

18th Thursday

"For he hath put all things under his feet. But when he saith all things are put under him, it is manifest that he is exempted, which did put all things under him."

1 Cor. 15: 27.

Under His feet

The heel is important in spiritual warfare. It is the organ for spiritual expression. The heel is what imparts our spiritual force when he demonstrates our will. It is with the heel that evil men betray and strikes the righteous; Ps 41: 9; *"Yea, mine own familiar friend, in whom I trusted, which did eat of my bread, hath lifted up his heel against me."* It is also with the heel that the righteous, crushes the demonic power of darkness; Gen 3: 15. While scripture says the power and vices of carriers of darkness would end under the feet of the righteous, it is with the feet that the righteous defeats and annihilates the wicked. What is the heel? It is the seat of supernatural power, knowledge and strength with which we fully discern, engage and defeat the forces of darkness. It is the active power, glory and authority of the anointing of Christ. Ask God for your heel that you have supernatural insight into the future. Ask God for the grace to predict new trend in business; favourable financial sources and a healthy family. Ask Him to put all things under your feet, by the same power with which he subdues all things; Col 1: 10-11; *"That ye might walk worthy of the Lord unto all pleasing, being fruitful in every good work, and increasing in the knowledge of God; strengthened with all might, according to his glorious power, unto all patience and longsuffering with joyfulness."*

Get hold of current trend in business and do great works by faith. 1 Cor. 15: 25-28, says; *"For he must reign, till he hath put all enemies under his feet. The last enemy that shall be destroyed is death. For he hath put all things under his feet. But when he saith all things are put under him, it is manifest that he is excepted, which did put all things under him. And when all things shall be subdied unto him, then shall the Son also himself be subject unto him that put all things under him, that God maybe all in all."* To put things under your feet means to reign. You must be in charge and command power. Secondly, you must be under subjection to Christ. You don't break the hedge and talk about putting things under your feet. That's rebellion. To put things under your feet means to be dependant on Christ and be full of the power of God.

Ask the Lord to favour your gracious course, ministerial counsel and business proposals today. How do you attain this? It is by being in God's presence; being led by the Holy Spirit. Reading and believing scriptures etc. You can start by doing the works of Christ in your immediate area of influence; like your office, home or church. Pray, work and help others attain their destinies by knowing their pains, challenges and limitations. When will you predict the times? When will you be able to get the predictions of your business right? When will you establish a blue-print of holy communication that's free of corruption? 1 Cor. 15: 33. Like Abraham, you are blessed in all things; Gen 24: 1; *"And Abraham was old, and well stricken in age: and the LORD had blessed Abraham in all things."*

Prayer line

Father Lord, give me a life-long power to serve you and prosper in business. Give me the capacity to transfer your protection, love and mercy, to my children; even as you make my bloodline triumphant citizens of the commonwealth, in Jesus name! Amen!

Further Study

Gen 27: 12, Ex 34: 21

19th Friday

"For this is he that was spoken of by prophet Esaias, saying, The Voice of one crying in the wilderness, prepare ye the way of the Lord, make his path straight."

Matt 3: 3

Fortify your voice

Your voice speaks for you in ministry, business, family life and areas you plan to do exploit in the Lord's vineyard. Your voice is the impact of your current achievements, and significant demonstration of spiritual power that leaves indelible mark in the hearts of men. Your voice is the worth of your work; 1 Cor. 3: 13- 15; *"Every man's work shall be made manifest; for the day shall declare it, because it shall be revealed by fire; and the fire shall try every man's work of what sort it is. If any man's work abide which he hath built thereupon, he shall receive a reward. If any man's work shall be burned, he shall suffer loss; but he himself shall be saved; yet so by fire."*

Because John baptized Jesus, and was the last of the prophets, the Lord taught that no one born of a woman, is greater than John; Matt 11: 11; *"Verily I say unto you, Among them that are born of women there hath not risen a greater than John the Baptist; notwithstanding he that is least in the Kingdom is greater than he."*

The achievements of John the Baptist is enunciated in Matt 11: 16-19. In these verses, the Lord described him as being ascetic according to the Jewish law, and yet not winning the hearts and minds of the religious leaders of his day. He compared him to His Ministry, where these same leaders refused to be converted. So that in either way, whether through the ascetic lifestyle of the law, or His doctrine of holiness, or power of faith; there have been no response or conversion either; Jon 1: 11; *"He came unto his own and his own received him not."*

Have you received the Lord into your life? If indeed you've received him, you will certainly be greater than John the Baptist. If you are greater than John the Baptist why are you in obscurity? Why are you afraid of new trend in your area of business? Learn to fortify your voice and take your place among great men. Be led by the Holy Spirit and depend on the reliability of scriptures; Rom 8: 14. Be filled with the Spirit; Eph 5: 17-18. Don't quench the Spirit; 1 Thes 5: 19. Command obedience in ministry, inspire good deeds in business, and convey undeniable charisma, intelligence and goodwill in your family. When Jesus died amidst the signs of an earth quake, impenetrable darkness, rent curtain in the temple, the centurion who supervised his execution, and stood at the foot of his cross and confessed that surely Jesus is the Son of God; Matt 27: 54.

Prayer line

Father Lord; I receive profound power to walk in divine Knowledge, understanding and wisdom. Give me the auction for greatness that I may excel above my fellows. Give me your glory for ashes, prosperity for poverty, mercy for sacrifice; and peace for war that I may excel in Jesus name! Amen!

Scriptural Study
Heb 11: 1-40, 1 Cor. 15: 3-26

20th Saturday

"And Naboth said to Ahab, The Lord forbid it me, that I should give the inheritance of my fathers unto thee."

1 Kings 21: 3

Know the price

As a Christian businessman or woman, you are an asset in the Kingdom of God. You have an enduring inheritance in Christ. Unless otherwise, you are called to sustain all kingdom engagement, without been seen or heard; so that you can be soaked and take your place in the mystery. Price is the value of something – what you pay for something that is worthwhile. The text above is the response Naboth gave King Ahab, when the King sought to buy his vineyard. Naboth named the price. The price was that the vineyard being an ancestral inheritance, couldn't be sold at any price.

As a shrewd businessman, the price you pay for the survival of your business, isn't the merely the cost of maintaining or running your business. It isn't such overheads like salaries of staff, rents on business premises, or even interests on loans. It is neither the expertise nor creative stamina you need to get the business going. It is the risk you bear, in order to get going. In Luke 17: 32, Jesus said; "Whosoever shall seek to save his life shall lose it; and whosoever shall lose his life shall preserve it." No one that put his hands on the plough and looks back is fit for the kingdom. Lots wife, looked back and truncated her freedom! My dear friend, the value of your business, financial decisions or overall vision in business, is to remain on top of your business, as soon as decides to bear risks, in order to go up, and continue in business. Risk is what determines whether a business is worth the piece of paper on which it is written.

When I left a branch of my church and decided to set up a new branch, the church secretary told me to remember my toils, pains and anguish, when I built the former church and not abandon it. He didn't tell me the church strength is little, it has no equipment or that it is not capable of supporting me. He talked about my sufferings, toils and endless fasting and prayers that lavished on it to cause it to grow. That's the price I paid for building that church. It is also the worth of the church before God; Rev 2: 19.

When you apply for a loan from your bankers, and are given conditions that you are required to meet, you must look at the risk in your business, before you consider the profitability of your business. Sometimes, bankers, creditors and financial experts, won't give transparent financial considerations, if they think your proposal, despite its plausibility, may engender risks than profits. The fact that you are credit-worthy, and can pay back these loans, doesn't matter. What matters are that the business is full of risks may ruin your projected expectations. In which case, such business proposal can't be considered. You may have so much money in the bank to finance a dashing business proposal, yet your managers, bankers or insurers; will advice you not to invest a dime on your proposed investment and the proposal will fail. That's why your ability to bear risks, your capacity to indemnify your financers, your overall vision of a particular business or assurances of huge profit-making opportunities determines the viability of your business.

Prayer

Father Lord, grant me the rewards of my sufferings, and let it be with resounding testimonies in my business and ministry. I refuse to suffer in vain and be subject to the dictates of the wicked. I believe your word which says affliction shall not arise a second time. I receive power to sing a new song today, in the name of Jesus! Amen!

Further Study
Ps 119: 9, Col 1: 21-29.

21st Sunday

"Who shall separate us from the love of Christ? Shall tribulation, or distress, or persecution, or famine, or nakedness, or peril, or sword?"

Rom 8: 35

Forge ahead

No matter how long your sieges of losses are in business, you are urgently required to forge ahead by faith, and bear all the risks. There is a huge price for overcoming obstacles; 2 Cor. 4: 14; *"Knowing that he which raised up the Lord Jesus shall raise up us also by Jesus, and shall present us with you.*" Faith is the way out of any catastrophe. Bearing risks is the soul of business and the compass of ministry. Even though it is heart-breaking to fail in life, it is far worse not to bear risks. We bear risks in business, ministry or any enterprise, when we are able to use what we don't see, to replace and utterly replicate what we see; 1 Cor. 1: 28; *"And base things of the world, and things which are despised, hath God chosen, yea, and things which are not, to bring to nought things that are."* The proposals may not be profit-oriented, yet we see huge profits through the eyes of faith. That's how we end up on the other side of the clan of achievers, and make mouth-watering profits, from our investments. We believe we can and find we have netted a fortune.

When we believe in Jesus, we are going to face serious risks. Therefore we should be ready to bear those risks and weather the storm. The Lord warned in countless scriptures that it will be very, very tough. Jesus didn't say, when you believe in Him; it will be smooth- sailing, or that you will eat sumptuous meals, sleep on an ivory bed and ride custom made limousines. These will come at the end but the beginning will be very tough; Mk 10: 29-30; *"And Jesus answered and said, verily I say unto you, There is no man that hath left house, or brethren, or sisters, or father, or mother, or wife, or children, or lands, for my sake, and the gospel's, But he shall receive an hundredfold now in this time, houses, and brethren, and sisters, and mothers, and children, and lands, with persecutions; and in the world to come eternal life."*

Prayer line

Father Lord, I receive power to endure to the end that I maybe saved. I receive the staying power of the Holy Spirit and the assurances of my salvation, deliverance and breakthroughs in the name of Jesus! Amen!

Further Study
James 2: 25, Heb 12: 12

22nd Monday

"Strive to enter in at the strait gate: for many, I say unto you, will seek to enter in, and shall not be able."

Lk 13: 24

Aspects of the price

Meditate on the price you are going to pay and be ready. The price is a lifelong sacrifice. In Matt 22: 1-13, a King did a wedding feast for his son and threw the door open to all men with just one condition that all guests should put on the weeding garment. Despite this easy condition, when he came in to greet his guests, he found a man who came in without a wedding garment, and said unto him:.." *how camest thou in hither without a wedding garment? And he was speechless."* We must ensure that we pay the price as it is the least condition for our eternal redemption.

Some aspects of the price you will have to pay are listed as follows.

- You will be requested to forsake the world and her immoral and lusty indulgencies throughout your life; 1 John 2: 15-17.You will have to confront lust and corruption at the pain of death; 2 Pet 1: 4.This is serious and must be obeyed to the end. Any attempt to go back to the world after you have been born again is an act of profanity. It is crucifying Christ a second time and toiling with your eternal damnation.

- You will be persecuted night and day, and become an adept of spiritual warfare; Eph 6: 10-18. Those that will fight you will be members of your household, so you can't harm them; Matt 10: 38. Be ready therefore, as this will certainly break your heart, and cause you to adjust your outlook for you to survive in life, ministry and business.

- You will be required to be on the cross perpetually; James 1:12. You will learn to be dead in your body, and be alive in the spirit, in order to survive; Matt 24: 13.

- You will become an object of judgment; a platform for measuring truth; 1 Cor. 6: 2-7. This will strain your relationship with people, including your spouse and children.

- The boundary, requirements and other details that you will get from the Holy Spirit, will confine you to the personality of Christ; Phil 2: 5-10.

- You will be requested by God to win souls at your personal peril; Matt 10: 32-33.

- Your desire will be to have eternal fellowship with God; Phil 1: 21-24.

Sometimes, the need to pay the price, may come from unsuspected angles, like a spouse, as was the case of Job; or from people that are part of the suffering, anguish and hurt, you have to bear in order to survive. In which case, the price may not be predictable; Job 2: 9; *"Then said his wife unto him, Dost thou still retain thine integrity? Curse God and die."* Job's three friends, accused him of heinous sins against God, but Job stood his grounds and pleaded his innocence.

At the end of his sufferings, God commended Job; and disapproved of his friends. When Paul's critical disciple left him in the midst of a turbulent ministry, he felt it; 2 Tim 4: 10; *"For Demas hath forsaken me, having loved this present world, and is departed unto Thessalonica; Cresence to Galatia, Titus unto Dalmatia."*

Prayerline

Father Lord, I receive the grace to bear the afflictions, shame and troubles of the cross, that I may fulfill my calling that's in Christ. Lord, fill me with divine power that I may rejoice greatly in all my endeavours today in Jesus name! Amen!

Further Study
Rom 5: 6, Acts 19: 13-20

23rd Tuesday

"But I have a few things against thee, because thou hast there them that hold the doctrine of Balaam, who taught Balac to cast a stumbling block before the children of Israel, to eat things sacrificed unto idols, and to commit fornication."

Rev 2: 14

Balm

The balm of Gilead is a term often used for the healing potency of Christ; Jer. 8: 22; *"Is there no balm in Gilead; is there no physician there? Why then is not the health of the daughter of my people recovered?"* Jesus asked similar questions in Luke 4: 23-30. The Balm is more of the goodwill, grace and manifestation of God that's demonstrated in the healing virtues of the Holy Spirit. It is one of the needs of any Christian businessman that insures him against losses, and endears him to high business profitability; Matt 5: 4-16. You must share in this special ability, provided by the balm, for you to excel in business and be endeared to all.

The term also refers to the life-giving power of the Lord Jesus Christ that is available by faith in those who believe. You are therefore requested to tap into this life-giving power of the Lord, in other to have clear oversight of your ministerial calling. The balm is what showcases your nature, skill or ability, as a peace-builder, facilitator of grace, and a minister of justice. You are become the epitome of truth, faithfulness and consistency. With it you can't be associated with evil; fraud or dubiety. You become addicted to the vocation of Christ with all gravity, and are equipped to fight the good fight.

Your business is the platform where you are requested to fight the battle of the ancients. Put on your war-gear therefore and be ready to fight. In order to win in this war, you must be grounded in the doctrine of Christ that operates on the goodwill of God, and reflect it in your professional practice, as an anointed Christian businessman. Eschewing double standards as Balaam did, who sneaked out of his home to curse the children of Israel because of the rewards of divination and love for money; 2 Pet 2: 15: *"Which have forsaken the right away, and are gone astray, following the way of Balaam the son of Bosor, who loved the wages of unrighteous; But was rebuked for his iniquity; the dumb ass speaking with man's voice forbad the madness of the prophet."*

Prayer line

Father Lord, cover my family, business and ministry with your mighty wings of redemption, salvation and deliverance. Let your anointing of unique power, prosperity and abundant life, reign in me. Open my eyes to powerful business opportunities today, that I may testify to your goodness in Jesus name! Amen!

Further Study

Lk 4: 18-19, Jon 4: 31-34

24th Wednesday

"There cometh a woman of Samaria to draw water: Jesus saith unto her, Give me to drink."

Jon 4: 7

Neighbourliness

Break down barriers that strangulate the flow of the Holy Spirit, and you will find favors from unlikely quarters. Put Samaritans or people that desire attention, care and love, on your watch list and expend your time, care and wherewithal to support them. Jesus did this, when he asked a Samaritan woman, to give him water to drink. Being a Jew, this was forbidden under orthodox Jewish laws. The Jews for racial reasons, felt more superior than a Samaritan. This complex bred national hatred, suspicion and needless tensions between Jews and Samaritans. The Lord Jesus destroyed this barrier in the course of this encounter with the woman; Jon4: 9; *"Then saith the woman of Samaria unto him, How is it that thou, being a Jew, askest drink of me, which am a woman of Samaria? For the Jews have no dealings with the Samaritans."*

Read the parable of the good Samaritan and destroy every form of social classification that is limiting your outreach programmes in church or business. Do this and be refreshed with smashing testimonies. Consider the story of the good Samaritan; Lk 10: 30- 36; *"And Jesus answering said, a certain, man went down from Jerusalem to Jericho, and fell among thieves, which stripped him of his raiment, and wounded him, and departed, leaving him half dead. And by chance there came down a certain priest that way; and when he saw him, he passed by on the other side. And likewise a Levite, when he was at the place, came and looked on him, and passed by on the other side. But a certain Samaritan, as he journeyed, came where he was. When he saw him, he had compassion on him, and went to him, and bound up his wounds, pouring in oil and wine, and set him on his own beast, and brought him to an inn, and took care of him. And on the morrow when he departed, he took out two pence, and gave them to the host, and said unto him, Take care of him; and whatsoever thou spendest more, when I come again, I will repay thee. Which now of these three, thinkest thou, was neigbour unto him that fell among the thieves."*

Be persistent in doing good; ask, seek and knock; Matt 7: 7. Don't build mental walls of racial or intellectual discrimination. Don't despise anyone. Avoid regrettable acts of exclusion, repression, victimization and needless restrictions around your business. Let the Lord lead you where ever you wish to go, and learn to enjoy the flow of God's mercy. Many lose divine opportunities, blessings and goodwill, by not stepping out of their insipid shells, or brazen self-made walls they built around their lives. They become stagnated, opinionated and dread the unknown.

Prayer line

Father Lord, teach me the mystery of good neighbourliness that I may walk under the spread of your divine power, today. Let me be at peace with my neighbours; use me to bless as many that will come my way today, in Jesus name! Amen!

Further Study
Pro 14: 31, James 1: 27

25th Thursday

"Now I beseech you brethren, by the name of our Lord Jesus Christ, that ye all speak the same thing, and that there be no divisions among you; but that ye be perfectly joined together in the same mind and in the same judgment."

1 Cor. 1: 10

Loath divisions

Study these steps that will enable you avoid divisions in your family, business and church.

- Divisions are contrary to Christian doctrine, as a divided house cannot stand; Cor. 1: 10; *"Now I beseech you, brethren, by the name of the Lord Jesus Christ, that ye all speak the same thing, and that there be no divisions among you; but that ye be perfectly joined together in the same mind and in the same judgement."*

- Reconcile divisions immediately as soon as they appear, otherwise there may be huge cracks that will affect the prosperity of the family, staff or ministry. Reconcile divisions by identifying and reaffirming the mandates of your business or ministry; 1 Cor. 1: 17; *"For Christ sent me not to baptize, but to preach the gospel; not with wisdom of words, lest the cross of Christ should be made of none effect."*

- Treat everyone equally. When you do that you establish peace and pursue the ideals for which the church or business was established; Mk 10: 44; *"And whosoever of you will be chiefest, shall be servant of all."*

- Teach, demonstrate and impart love in your staff, family members or church workers; Rom 13: 8; *"Owe no man anything; but to love one another: for he that loveth another hath fulfilled the law."*

- Encourage giving, create a welfare fund to circulate among members of your family, business and church staff; Luke 6: 38.

Prayer line

Father Lord, take away every strange power that's causing divisions, strife and separation in my family, business and ministry; unite my family, business and ministry that everyone may see from same perspective, mind and belief in the name of Jesus! Amen!

Further Study
Matt 12: 25, Rom 1: 16

26th Friday

"Then Jesus said unto them, My time is not yet come: but your time is always ready."

Jon 7: 6

Return another time

Sometimes, the only way to survive in business or in ministry, is do what David did, when he discovered that he would one day perish in the hands of King Saul; 1 Sam 27: 1; *"And David said in his heart, I shall now perish one day by the hand of Saul: there is nothing better for me than that I should speedily escape into the land of the Philistines; and Saul shall despair of me, to seek me any more in any coast of Israel: so shall I escape out of his hand."*

Learn to flee the scene of any conflict when its dangerous, and return some other time; Matt 10:23; *"But when they persecute you in this city, flee ye into another: for verily I say unto you, Ye shall not have gone over the cities of Israel, till the Son of Man be come."* Be flexible in your wrestling, and not snap under a needless weight. Avoid danger and don't court trouble. In order to escape from his imminent destruction, David sought refuse in the land of the Philistines; Israel most bellicose enemy. You are entitled to all the resources in the universe. The Earth is the Lord's and its fullness thereof. Avoid this: don't erect barriers of language, race, ethnicity and kindred or clan hate, as it will limit you of your strategic benefits and breakthroughs.

You must be conscious of the presence of God and strive to obey Him by faith; Rom 8: 14. Victory is measured by how close we are to God at the moment, and not our past acts of faith. In order to have all round victories, avoid what would make you not hear the leading of the Holy Spirit. The following are things you have to do, in order to be fortified and led by the Holy Spirit.

- You must be in the presence of God to be led; Eph 2: 18. Once in God's presence, His glory will be imputed on you, and you will defeat the forces of darkness.
- Live one day at a time; re-strategize and change your time-consciousness to suit His eternal times and seasons; James 4: 13-15.
- Be heavenly-minded; look heavenward, in holy conversation; Col 3: 13.
- Apply the word consciously and experience the defeat of darkness. Remember that the word is the sword of the Spirit; Heb 4: 12. Be practical. Your victory is calculated by how deep you fellowship with God, out of a pure and sincere heart; Matt 5: 8; *"Blessed are the pure in heart: for they shall see God."*
- Live in full demonstration of gifts, fruits and ministerial functions; Gal 5: 16; *"This I say then, walk in the Spirit, and ye shall not fulfill the lust of the flesh."*

Prayer line

Father Lord, fortify and divinely equip me for breakthroughs today. Cause me to be led by your precious Holy Spirit in Jesus name! Amen!

Further Study

Ps 70: 1, Deut 32: 21

27thSaturday

"Hast not thou made an hedge about him, and about his house, and about all that he hath on every side? Thou hast blessed the work of his hands, and his substance is increased in the land."

Job 1: 10

The hedge

A hedge is when you exercise victory over demonic forces. You are expected to bear witness of the hedge all the time, and be sure of your sanctification and overall deliverance. The hedge is also when you enforce your right of son-ship over a given problem and through this, enjoy the reward of exemption from affliction or loss.

The story of Daniel in Nebuchadnezzar's fiery furnace proves the reality of the Hedge, as a spiritual shield in the life of believers. The decision by Daniel not to eat the King's meat, invested him with spiritual power and made him invincible; Dan 1: 8.The crack-team fellowship that supervised his defenses, sustained itself with deliverance prayers that brought the glory of God upon him. The Hedge is broken by defilements from idolatrous food (eating in dreams), from adultery (the type that ruined the Shield of David), and point blank idolatry, like that type the Moabites invented; Num 25: 1. *"And Israel abode in Shittim, and the people began to commit whoredom with the daughters of Moab. And they called the people into the sacrifices of their gods: and the people did eat and bowed down to their gods. And Israel joined himself unto baalpeor and the anger of the lord was kindled against Israel"*

Beware of idolatry, adultery, fornication or fetish festivals; they have power to break the Hedge that's over you and your family, and make you susceptible to devourers. The Jezebel Spirit is empowered to break the Hedge of unsuspecting men, when Jezebelic women seduce them, and bring them under demonic control. Jesus lamented over the relentless targeting of His servants by the Jezebelic spirits; Rev 2: 18. You must be conscious of Jezebelic attack and fight strenuously to defeat it.

The Hedge is also the target of false prophets. When the Moabites couldn't curse the children of Israel, because of the power of the Hedge over her, Balaam a false prophet, devised another means to break the Hedge. He asked the Moabites to send women of easy virtue into the camp of Israel, so that the men of Israel would commit fornication with them. Besides this that they may worship idols, and eat foods offered to idols. This had the effect of defiling them. The Lord abandoned Israel and the combined effect of a plague and God's anger killed more than 30, 000 men! The Hedge is built when we separate ourselves from unbelievers. It is broken when we mingle with them and are defiled. The Hedge is a fulfillment of God's promise to believers; Matt 28: 19.

Prayer line

Father Lord, I decree that because you are my God, my saviour and great deliverer, no one shall pluck me out of your hands today, neither shall anyone deny me of my blessings in Jesus name! Amen!

Further Study
Jon 10: 30, Job 5: 24

28th Sunday

"He suffered no man to do them wrong: yea, he rebuked Kings for their sakes; saying touch not my anointed, and do my prophets no harm."

Psalm 105: 14-15

The Lord will fight

When David faced Goliath, he told King Saul that the Lord who delivered him from the lion and bear, that he once killed, will also deliver him from Goliath. The Lord Jesus who is our eternal deliverer hasn't changed. That's why scripture says; Jesus Christ today, yesterday and forever; Heb 13: 8. God is very faithful to believers. The Lord fought for David and within an hour, he killed Goliath and became a national celebrity. He emerged from obscurity, and took center-stage as a future leader of Israel. The essence of your experience in business is for you to use it to create new areas of divine contacts, and demonstrate your sense of dependency on God.

Your experience in business should create proposals with higher digits in profit margin. Move from being a mediocre to being outstanding. Move from being a millionaire, to being a billionaire. Tell God your mind; your heart desire and he will bring you into the limelight of your business. Faith covers your tracts, mistakes, lack of insights and judgment. It is what you need in order to enter your glorious moments of divine breakthroughs. Yes. God's thoughts towards you are glorious and designed to make you outstanding.

When the children of Israel encamped on the banks of the Red Sea, they sensed danger and began to think how to cross it. To wander round it will take more than 100 years. To compound their problem, the Egyptians attacked them from the rear while they were surrounded by mountain ranges on their left side and right side that made escape impossible. The only passage out of the *cul de sac* was the red sea. Unknown to them, God was going to lead them through the red sea. The tension that this generated was heart-breaking. The Israelites panicked, cried and wailed.

They gathered around Moses and vented their frustration in a manner that showed how faithless they were. They allowed their fear of death, to destroy their faith in God. Moses obeyed the instructions God gave him in stages. He suddenly had an insight to move forward. He walked up to the banks of the Red Sea and said what changed the perception of the danger they faced; Ex 15: 13-14; *"Moses said unto the people, fear ye not, stand still, and see the salvation of the LORD, which he will show to you today: for the Egyptians whom ye have seen today, ye shall see them again no more for ever! And the Lord shall fight for you, and ye will hold your peace."*

Prayer

Father Lord, fight my enemies and scatter them that they may not be able to withstand me. Fill them with grief, tribulation, anxiety and self-destruction. Let my cause become just, clear and shiny, like the midday sun. I refused to be punished with the wicked, in Jesus name! Amen!

Further Study

Num 10: 35, Ps 16: 10

29th Monday

"And he entreated Abram well for her sake: and he had sheep, and oxen, and he asses, and maidservants, and maid servants, and she asses, and camels."

Gen 12: 16

Wealth from unlikely quarters

You must understand that a mystery surrounds the wealth of the children of God. God is their wealth; Col 2: 3. Abraham became rich, when he got favour for not withholding Sarah from an intrusive King of Egypt called Abimelech; Gen 20: 2; 12: 14-20. The anguish Abraham endured created a financial leeway for the great man. What was a tragic mistake became a financial favour-spinner. What he thought had gone awry created avenues for deliverance and protection of the godly family; Gen 20: 6; *"And God said unto him in a dream, yea, I know that thou didst this in the integrity of thy heart; for I also withheld thee from sinning against me: therefore suffered I thee not to touch her."*

The Egyptian King called Abimelech in Gen 20: 6, encountered God in a vision and was amazed at the simplicity and meekness of Abram; Matt 11: 29. God brought him under divine scrutiny that broke his hardened nature; Gen 12: 17-18; *"And the LORD plagued pharaoh and his house with great plagues because of Sarai Abrams's wife. And Pharaoh called Abram, and said what is this that thou hast done unto me? Why didst thou not tell me that she was thy wife?"*

God commanded him to restore Sarai and disclosed that Abraham was a prophet; Gen 20: 7. Abraham prayed for the King and his household and healed them; Gen 20: 17.This penitent question marked a season of gracious favour that Abraham enjoyed throughout his life; Gen 12: 20. Then Pharoah commanded his men concerning Abram and he empowered him financially, and broke his pathetic stagnation. God extolled Abram as a prophet and pleaded his cause before Abimelech; Gen 20: 7-8. This shattered the King and he surrendered his will to Abram. In Gen 13: 2, Abram became very rich; *"And Abram was very rich in cattle, in silver, and in gold. "*He got his wealth from unlikely quarters. That will be your portion this last day of the month.

Prayer

Father Lord, cause me to encounter your favour in multiple financial breakthrough this month; let your favour come from unlikely sources that men may know I serve a living God, in Jesus name, Amen!

Further Study

1Kings 10: 24-25; 1 Sam 2: 8-10

Acknowledgements

I graciously acknowledge and seek the kind permission of the following sources, for illustrations used in this devotional.

home.howstuffworks.com
madefreshly.com
www.reliefshading.com
www.zteusa.com
leftyconcarne.wordpress.com
www.graphics20.com
fractkali.deviantart.com
nature.desktopnexus.com
www.dreamsleep.net
www.pracbrown.co.uk
www.fighttime.net
www.businessinsider.com
www.constantinealexander.net
galleryhip.com
automobilein.com
blogontheuniverse.org
voiceofrevival.ca
www.morgan.edu
forum.worldoftanks.eu
www.feasta.org
www.yourart.com
www.danpink.com
www.huffingtonpost.co.uk
www.goldprincipal.com
www.engadget.com
troyjr24.deviantart.com
home.howstuffworks.com
madefreshly.com

www.reliefshading.com
www.zteusa.com
leftyconcarne.wordpress.com
www.graphics20.com
fractkali.deviantart.com
nature.desktopnexus.com
www.dreamsleep.net
www.pracbrown.co.uk
www.fighttime.net
www.businessinsider.com
www.constantinealexander.net
galleryhip.com
automobilein.com
The Final Countdown: Shuttle Atlantis Soars Heavenward
for Last ...
blogontheuniverse.org
voiceofrevival.ca
www.morgan.edu
forum.worldoftanks.eu
www.feasta.org
www.yourart.com
www.danpink.com
www.huffingtonpost.co.uk
www.goldprincipal.com
www.engadget.com
troyjr24.deviantart.com
www.onlineuniversities.com

skills

rt.com

money

www.colourbox.com

vegetable salad

scales 1 -
http://www.wpclipart.com/holiday/election_Day/scales ...
www.wpclipart.com
I'm Major: One Scale That Won't Get You Down |
AbletonTutorials ...
www.anthonyarroyodotcom.com468 × 481Search by image
I'm Major: One Scale That Won't Get You Down
www.referenceforbusiness.com420 × 420Search by image
mspmentor.net
aruhat.com
www.heartbeatexperts.com406 × 262Search by image
Pricing and Reimbursement
Otto Dix: MatthausEvangelium
bowdencollections.com576 × 372Search by image
Clip Art Vector of A riverbank with flowers and a rainbow
...
www.canstockphoto.com450 × 451Search by image
A riverbank with flowers and a rainbow - csp15439
Digging in with SmartBear's API Tools
blog.smartbear.com
blogography.com420 × 319Search by image
DAVETOON: Lil' Dave Digging a Hole
arabianindustry.com
Twelve die in Saudi and UAE labour camp blazes ...
www.constructionweekonline.com
Marine Life Props Add-On | BirthdayExpress.com
www.birthdayexpress.com1600 × 1600Search by image
Marine Life Props Add-On

Pricingwww.forbes.com
wisesyracuse.wordpress.com

www.webdefensesystems.com300 × 300Search by image

mspmentor.net

aruhat.com

www.heartbeatexperts.com406 × 262Search by image

Pricing and Reimbursement

Otto Dix: Matthaus Evangelium

bowdencollections.com576 × 372Search by image

Coin in the Mouth of the Fish

Clip Art Vector of A riverbank with flowers and a rainbow
...

www.canstockphoto.com450 × 451Search by image

A riverbank with flowers and a rainbow - csp15439

Digging in with Smart Bear's API Tools

blog.smartbear.com

blogography.com420 × 319search by image

davetoon: lil' dave digging a hole

arabianindustry.com

Twelve die in Saudi and UAE labour camp blazes ...

www.constructionweekonline.com

Marine Life Props Add-On | BirthdayExpress.com

www.birthdayexpress.com1600 × 1600Search by image

Marine Life Props Add-
On.

Deep Blue Marine Life by Charles Stuart - Deep Blue
Marine Life ...

fineartamerica.com600 × 253Search by image

Deep Blue Marine Life Painting

Oberon's Grove:

oberon481.typepad.com1600 × 1000Search by image

Martha Graham: Myth & Transformation II

www.ingramcontent.com/pod-product-compliance
Lightning Source LLC
Chambersburg PA
CBHW032018170526
45157CB00002B/749